Learning Little Hawk's Way of Storytelling

Learning Little Hawk's Way of Storytelling

by
Kenneth Little Hawk
and Beverly Miller
as taught to
Frank Domenico Cipriani

FINDHORN PRESS

Published by Findhorn Press in 2011

ISBN 978-1-84409-536-0

A CIP record for this title is available from the British Library.

Edited by Shari Mueller
Interior design by Thierry Bogliolo
Front cover design by Richard Crookes
Printed and bound in the USA

Published by

Findhorn Press
117-121 High Street,
Forres IV36 1AB,
Scotland, UK
t +44 (0)1309 690582
f +44 (0)131 777 2711
e info@findhornpress.com
www.findhornpress.com

Contents

Discovering Little Hawk

I am blessed with a good friend, named Barbara, who keeps bringing wonderful people into my life. One day, Barbara urged me to go to the local library and watch the performance of an amazing Storyteller, Kenneth Little Hawk, who is Mi'kmaq/Mohawk and a member of the Métis Eastern Tribal Indian Society of Maine.

That storytelling experience was unforgettable as were the subsequent ones I attended with my children. It was as if Little Hawk spoke for Mother Earth herself, that his lessons came from somewhere beyond the brick walls and concrete floors of the library. In his flute music and his stories about our connectedness to all things, Little Hawk was translating the voices of the wind through the cedar swamps and the cries of the cicada and whippoorwill into a language that we all understood but had forgotten to heed. As I was running an outdoor primitive survival camp for local children, including my own four, we couldn't wait for Little Hawk and his marvelous storytelling talents to bring us lessons of respect for one another and the Earth.

When I approached Grandfather Little Hawk and Grandmother Beverly with the idea of holding a storytelling workshop for children, Little Hawk's initial reaction was, "But I don't claim to be a teacher. I'm a Storyteller." What strange words coming from a man who regularly visits libraries and schools, and whose stories have been part of university curriculum! As we worked together on that first workshop, I began to understand what he meant. The stories teach, not the Storyteller.

Watching this husband and wife communicate their lessons, I witnessed the special relationship that connects a great Storyteller and Caretaker to their audience. The Storyteller isn't a celebrity, someone whose life is separated from his audience by silver screens and velvet ropes. A Storyteller is someone who guides each listener to understand his/her own value. Somehow, at the end of every Little Hawk performance I ever witnessed, the audience members came away feeling more positively about themselves, and therefore inspired to direct their lives towards the simple lessons the stories taught about living in a good way.

This book is based on Little Hawk's own family stories. It includes original stories created by Little Hawk, retold First Nations' stories and the lessons of our storytelling workshops. We drew upon the insightful analysis of Beverly. Then I researched the language, early history, and culture of one of the most admirable civilizations the world has ever known, the Mi'kmaq. When I presented my writing to Little Hawk and Beverly, their comments and rewrites were always wise, and always connected to the trust and the sense of integrity with which they regarded each of you, our dear readers.

While my job was to create a portion of the body of this work, Beverly and Little Hawk provided the foundation for spirit, mind, and ideas to come together as one. We are pleased that Findhorn Press, with its wonderful mission of delivering life-changing books to the world, is our publisher. The people at Findhorn Press have guided us through this process with patience and an appreciation of the higher purpose we hoped to achieve by creating this book.

We three authors have dedicated our lives to the ancient and sacred storytelling traditions and have delved deeply into First Nations' lore. I was always excited to see the changes Little Hawk and Beverly made to this work. The pair have such a wonderful ability to find meaning in the dense jungles of my prose. By the end of this process, I felt I had received an education that perfectly paralleled the lessons Many Smiles learned about storytelling.

The three of us played. We played with the names of the characters, we played with the plot line, we spent many hours laughing. I have rarely met two people more in touch with their inner children than these two septuagenarians.

They also lifted my understanding. They respected me enough to let me know where the imperfections in my writing lay. As experienced and wise as they are, they were always willing to learn from me as well.

They told the truth, always bravely and kindly.

Perhaps most importantly, just as they do in their storytellings, they took care that every line they wrote, every correction, every insight would fill these pages with love.

Now this book has come to your hands. I am personally fascinated to see what you can do with the lessons provided here. We encourage you to join our Facebook fan group, record your stories and post them to our pages, so we may share them. The world of storytelling has come full circle, and though many miles may separate us, technology allows us to have a personal relationship with all of you who share our passion for storytelling.

From my heart, here is my wish for you all: May your stories continue to be told, seven generations from now, so that your great, great, great, great grandchildren may live in a good way.

—*Frank Domenico Cipriani*

One

From the Heart of Little Hawk

You are about to become a Storyteller, taken on a journey through time. You will be born as a child once again, spending time in the joyful heart of your childhood. You will grow into a Storyteller as a seed grows into a tree.

People have written many books on the subject of storytelling. They are very good. They teach technique and explain the purpose of storytelling. Authors explain that one of the most powerful purposes of storytelling is to teach. This caused me to wonder—if an author believes in the power of telling a story to teach a lesson, why doesn't he or she teach storytelling by using this wonderful method? This book does just that…it teaches storytelling by telling a story.

People might ask if this book is fiction or nonfiction. Is this book for adults or for children? These stories can be read on many levels. They can be read to entertain, to teach culture and living in a good way, to illustrate a respectful relationship with the Earth and with each other, or they can be used to learn the ancient art of storytelling. This can be considered a "how-to" book or a book of fiction for people of any age. These stories are carefully selected to teach you—the way Grandmother and Grandfather taught me—the lessons that you will need to learn to become a Storyteller.

I have told stories to people from all walks of life—from toddlers to elders in their nineties and above—and they responded warmly and encouragingly. To me, stories are living things that spring from the Earth's own story, from the changing of seasons, and they grow over time like trees dropping seeds to feed the future generations.

My hope is to share stories with you that will help you learn to tell stories. Your challenge is to find the lessons in the stories. It isn't difficult. Like the stories themselves, this book can be read many times, and each time you may find new lessons in the stories. Each story has at least one basic, one intermediate, and one advanced lesson covering ways of storytelling. You are invited to invent exercises and practices based on each tale told. Each time you read a story using your desire to become a Storyteller in the oral tradition, you will become a better Storyteller.

If you are picking up this book for the first time, I will help you get started with a direct assignment. Your goal is to become the sound of the drum and the smile on people's faces—just like the character, Startle Drumming/Many Smiles—and to learn the lessons in those sounds and feelings.

Grandmother and Grandfather would tell me stories; that was my way of learning—that was the way I was taught many lessons to help guide me in a good way. But it may not be the way of most of my readers. Giving direct instruction is a process used in many of the books today. Therefore, for those who feel more comfortable with a curriculum, I have included assignments in Section 6 of this book that will show you how to read the book again and again to learn new lessons. The rest of you will get little direct instruction except for what is now said: the first time you read this book, read it to yourself just as you would read any book. If, along the way, you find suggestions, crafts, and exercises—anything that you might want to try for yourself—let the book inspire you to try these things.

I suggest that, whenever you hold this book, you thank the trees who have helped to share these words provided in the pages of this book. When the trees lie down upon the Earth, they feed the forest. And after many years they become tiny pieces of Grandmother Rock and have many stories to share. We call upon Grandmother Rock and the ancestors and friends who have lived on Earth who wished the best for future generations, and upon whose lives our lives are built. It is with gratitude we ask them to teach us and show us the way.

If you are reading this book for the second time, please read it aloud in your own many voices. By now, you may have a storytelling pebble and a pouch to place it in. Make sure to play with this stone and pouch as you read each story aloud, and notice the lessons you learn. Compare the story in your imagination to the story told in your actual voice. Don't be afraid to use exaggerated expressions as you speak. Imagine you are telling the stories to a small child.

The third time you read this book, please focus on the fact that these stories are meant to be read outdoors. Read them to the clouds and to the insects. Read them back to the rocks from which they sprung. Read as if nobody's listening, the way most people sing in the shower.

Then the fourth time you tell these stories, please tell them to another Storyteller. The Storyteller could even be a child or a person in a nursing home. Such tales are best read to someone who has shed inhibition and has time to listen.

When you tell these stories for a fifth time, tell them to a larger group. Pay close attention to what these stories teach about arranging people in a room, about making the people move, about filling available space.

Then, tell the stories to people who can't understand your native language! This is a wonderful challenge, one I have had occasion to practice when I tell stories in other countries or when I am in front of an audience where some of my listeners are deaf. If you cannot find people like this, tell these stories in your own made-up language and rely on your body and voice for communication.

By the time you have told these stories six times, you will be ready to help other Storytellers, to tend their fires, to pass them their drums as you "read" the audience, and to communicate with these other Storytellers in a language of gesture and movement of which the audience isn't even aware.

Seven is a special number. It was a very important number to my Mi'kmaw grandmother. The Mi'kmaq have seven districts represented in our Grand Council, so in a sense, as you tell the stories seven times, imagine you are visiting seven different districts and learning from The People each time. My grandmother also taught me that each decision that is made should be considered for the impact it will have seven generations to come. Tell your stories knowing that someday your great-grandchildren's great-grandchildren will tell these same stories. And *who* are your children and grandchildren? *All* the children are your children and grandchildren.

According to my grandmother, the name Mi'kmaq comes from the way we referred to other people. When Our People met anyone—strangers or friends—we referred to them as *Ni'kmaq*, which means *my relative, my kins-man, my brother and sister*. This all-embracing acceptance is an important part of the philosophy I was taught and a key to understanding how to live in peace and harmony with Mother Earth.

This is the spirit of the word *Ni'kmaq* and I drew on the wisdom of my ancestors to write these words:

> *How would it be if you looked at me as Brother?*
> *How would it be if she looked at her as Sister?*
> *Elders as Grandmother and Grandfather*
> *And all the children as our own.*
> *How would it be if we looked at Earth as Mother?*
> *How would it be if we looked at Sky as Father?*
> *How would it be if we really cared for each other?*
> *The reason ancestors existed at all.*

My great-grandmother carried my grandmother South from Nova Scotia to the Catskills by buckboard and by cradleboard. The knowledge that was taught to my grandmother was taught to me.

"What did you learn in school today?" my grandmother would ask. She would add, "We have lessons, too. Listen."

Then she would tell me a story. I do not say that my words in this book contain all the storytelling traditions of my Mi'kmaw, Mohawk, and Shin-necock heritage. The traditions, characters, and stories in this book would have been familiar to Grandmother and Grandfather who were instrumen-tal in my early formation as a Storyteller. My voice is of their voice, not of *all* indigenous voices of North America. And my voice is in the spirit of Grandmother and Grandfather's voice that still echoes in me today: "Share what you can, as we have shared with you."

The wisdom of my elders still carries the essence of the storytelling: that all life is connected; all life is dependent on all life; and the treatment of life reveals the depths of our respect and compassion for the all-inclusive envi-ronment including plants, animals, rivers, and each other. As Grandmother and Grandfather said—and my many elders often repeated—"We are all one family, we just live on different parts of the Earth."

I have been privileged to have teachers in my early years who taught that sharing is a great gift. My words in this book are to respectfully honor my ancestors by sharing some of what life has taught me and to continue to see it with their eyes as much as still can be seen through mine.

Draw upon the wisdom Mother Earth offers each age, and share those stories in a good way.

From the earliest age, memory is recorded in every cell, laying the emotional foundation of the Storyteller.

From the age of childhood, Mother Earth teaches us to play and teaches us the stories of the ancestors.

From the age of self-discovery, we learn to relate to the listener's ability to understand and to let our story, their reactions, and the environment that surrounds us, speak to us as we speak to them. We call this *Lifting the Understanding*.

From the age of responsibility, we learn to fill the storytelling space with love.

From the age of strength, we learn to tell the truth.

From the age of slowing down, we learn how to carry a lighter burden.

From the age of wisdom, we learn how to tell just enough, move just enough, so that the story keeps playing in the mind of the listeners for the rest of their lives.

We thank our ancestors and Grandmother Rock who told stories to First Child. Just as all rocks descend from Grandmother Rock, we all descend from the same Great Spirit. We are all relatives.

First become familiar with the terms in the glossary. Then listen to the first story of a little boy who became a Storyteller. May you learn with him so that you, too, may become a Storyteller.

—*Kenneth Little Hawk*

Glossary

Bark Eaters: *Hatiroñ'āk*, this is a Mohawk word meaning "they eat bark". This is the name given to the tribe living in what is today the North Country of New York, from which the name Adirondack is derived.[1]

Bay of the Giant Beaver: Refers to a Glooscap story of creation where Glooscap breaks a giant beaver dam and creates the tides.

Chief: Not like a king, more like a first among equals, and a keeper of items collected by the village. This was never a hereditary title, but bestowed by consensus.

District Chief: Mi'kmaw territory was divided into seven districts. Each district had a District Chief, and each Chief was a member of the Grand Council.[2]

Dogbane: *Apocynum cannabinum*—also called Indian hemp, very useful plant for cordage.

Dulse: *Rhodymenia palmetta*—a delicious reddish seaweed which is a treat to eat dried or cooked.

Dyed moose hair: Moose hair can be naturally dyed red, green, blue or yellow. This was the preferred head decoration, not feathers.[3]

First Child: We adapted the story of the Storytelling Rock, which is a Seneca legend. First Child is sometimes known as First Boy. The rest of the stories of Grandmother Rock and First Child are stories we created to teach storytelling. Nothing historical, anthropological or cultural should be gleaned from them. This is a book on storytelling, not on ethnography.

Gift: Gift-giving traditions are much misunderstood by Europeans. In a society of limited possessions, a gift is a token of the quality, recognition of time, and talent given. Therefore, a gift could be a song, or some other token of respect. It does not necessarily mean the exchange of material items. It was called a "give away" and could not be refused. Such gifts were often valuable

Glooscap: To the European, Glooscap could be defined as the embodiment of understanding. This kind giant used knowledge to help and to teach The People. He plays a large role in Mi'kmaw storytelling.

Glooscap's Cave: Site of Glooscap's cave is Cape Breton Island at Cape Douphin.

Grandfather: Title of respect, not necessarily of kinship.

Grandmother Rock: It is clear that there was widespread communication amongst all North American people, allowing for the trade of wampum, tobacco, and permitting stories to be spread. This is a character from a Seneca tale, but it is possible that the Mi'kmaq would have heard it, if not directly from the Seneca, then from the Mohawk.[4]

Innu: These people live to the north of Nova Scotia and are related to the Cree. They traded with the Mi'kmaq and other tribes of the Wabanaki.[5]

Lenape: A tribe native to the Mid-Atlantic coast from the current state of Delaware to Southern New York, this was a peace-loving people, who like the L'nuk, moved from coastline to forest as the seasons changed.[6]

L'nuk: The word means *The People*, what the Mi'kmaq traditionally call themselves.

Marten: A member of the Mustelidae family, living in coniferous forests throughout the United States. A small weasel-like animal.

Mawiglulg: Means *it is very good* in *Míkmawísimk*, the language of the Mi'kmaq.

Mi'kmaq, Mi'kmaw: -q, plural, name of tribe -w, singular, or adjective describing the tribe.

Mikmwesúk: These tiny good-natured spirits would grow mischievous if disrespected, but were otherwise helpful and would assist The People with chores. They are only seen when they choose to be seen.[7]

Mohawk: Mohawk = *Kanien' kehake* (People of the Flint) part of the Iroquois Confederacy tribes living on the eastern border of Iroquoian speaking areas in the Northeast. It is conceivable that the Seneca tale of Grandmother Rock could have been related to the Wabanaki People through contact with the Mohawk.[8]

Moon of Berry Ripening: Corresponds to the month of August.[9]

Moose call: A birchbark "megaphone" through which The People would imitate the calls of the moose.[10]

Moose hunt and manhood: At the time of the moose hunt, the village was moved and the moose was driven towards the village. This required cooperation among hunters and non-hunters alike, and a deep understanding of the dynamics of both the Two-Legged and Four-Legged Nations. A young person who demonstrated this understanding was judged to have showed enough maturity to sit at the Council, to marry, and to become an adult.

Ni'kmaq: This means *my relative/kinfolk/friend*.

Northwind's wing: A legend that has, as many legends do, many forms. Basically, the Northwind bird flaps its wings to bring the cold, but brings too much cold. After not flapping at all, and causing great stagnation, a compromise is reached. Northwind flaps one wing (in some stories) or flaps with less intensity (in other stories).[11]

Pemmican: Cree word. Food which is a mixture of fats and protein, often with added dried fruit which can be stored for a season or more.[12]

Penobscot: Penobscot = *Panawahpskek*. Located in present-day Maine, one of the Wabanaki peoples. Penobscot share many traditions and stories with the Mi'kmaq.[13]

Puoin: An individual whose spiritual power could cure illness and protect people from harm.[14]

Purple Martin: A wide ranging migratory bird that travels between Brazil and the Northeast, it is known to devour biting flies. The Native Americans seem to have domesticated this bird thousands of years ago to the point that they now only live in man-made homes and never nest more than 120 yards from human habitation. They are very useful. They not only eat insects, but have very predictable seasonal behaviors and raise alarms at the approach of strangers and predators. The bird is even useful after its time. The dried meat of this bird repels moths.[15]

Quills: Using porcupine quills to decorate textiles is a common practice among First Nations of North America. Porcupine quills are dyed and sewn to leather or birchbark to form geometric designs and patterns. The significance of the "wrong color" in the quill work was that it reveals not only an imperfection, but possibly a sharp barb, which is always a darker color.[16]

Sea Mink: A wonderful large Mink of Nova Scotia, which the competitive European fur trade caused to be hunted to extinction by the 1860's. It was about twice the size of the American Mink.

Shinnecock: First Nation residents of eastern Long Island.

SNWE: A method of critiquing a piece.
S=South. The positive critique.
N=North. Point out one thing that could have gone better.
W=West. Say what can be done in the future.
E= Point out how the lessons from the past can help improve the piece.

Stories Facing East: For practical purposes, as well as spiritual ones, wigwam doors generally faced East. This being the case, revered storytelling elders sitting "high in the wigwam" would have been facing East to tell their stories. This, plus the fact that the Sun rises in the East make facing eastward while telling stories the preferred, but by no means exclusive way to face when storytelling.

Wabanaki: Abenaki, Maliseet, Passamaquoddy, Penobscot, Mi'kmaq[17], the five nations of The Wabanaki Confederacy referred to themselves as People of the Dawn. We presumed that even before the Confederacy, these tribes thought of themselves collectively as Children of the East, and shared a common ancestor. We use the term Wabanaki in this story to speak of the predecessors of these closely related people.[18]

Waltes: This is a game of chance played with six two-sided "dice" that are placed in a shallow hardwood bowl, which is slammed against the ground with sufficient force that the dice flip. Each die has a carved side and a plain side. To score, five or six of the dice must be flipped to matching sides. Counting sticks are used to keep score. When one person possesses all the counting sticks, that person wins.

Wiklatmu'j: Tiny creatures with rounded bodies and tiny arms and legs, as small as little children, but swift and unseen. They are generally friendly, but can cause mischief.[19]

1   http://www.accessgenealogy.com/native/tribes/a/adirondack_indian_history.htm
2   www.membertou400.com/events/cultural.village
3   Nativetech.org/weave/falseembroidery/index.html
4   http://reachstories.blogspot.com/2007/12/storytelling-stone-how-stories-began.html
5   http://en.wikipedia.org/wiki/Innu
6   http://www.lenapenation.org
7   http://www.newworldencyclopedia.org/entry/Passamaquoddy
8   www.Mohawktribe.com
9   http://micmac-nsn.gov/html/cultural_program.html
10   http://www.manataka.org/page259.html
11   http://www.firstpeople.us/FP-Html-Legends/Tumilkoontaoo-Or-The-Broken-Wing-Micmac.html
12   en.wikipedia.org/wiki/pemmican
13   En.wikipedia.org/wiki/Penobscot.people
14   www2.gnb.ca/content/GNB/EN/departments/aboriginal_affairs/wolastoqiyk/leaders.html
15   http://purplemartin.org/update/Indigenous.html
16   www.nativetech.org/weave/falseembroidery/index.html
17   http://www.wabanaki. /Harald_Prins.htm
18   www.wabanakinations.org/about.html
19   http://www.danielnpaul.com/Mi'kmaqCulture.html

Two

PLAY:

Lessons Learned in Childhood[1]

2.1 Childhood Before Memory:
Why a Child Becomes a Storyteller

This is the boy's first memory: Something is about to happen. The bark-covered walls of the tribal wigwam shift in shadow. The Grandparents sit deep in the wigwam close to the fire. The fire dances and jabs at the stars. The stars crowd the sky above the smokehole, twinkling with impatience as they look down and speak through the voice of the wind. The fire hisses and crackles, excited by what is about to happen. The Grandparents whisper and laugh with anticipation.

The fire lights up all the eager faces. The boy's younger uncles sit close to the entrance. The tall men sit with their legs crossed, and the women sit on their feet, so the women's heads are as high as the men's. All bodies lean

---

1   Refer to curriculum p.196–197

toward the door, all heads are turned. Some of the oldest boys and girls stand by the walls away from the fire. They look at each other and smile. Like the stars, their eyes twinkle with excitement. Our little boy, just four or five winters old, sits in his mother's warm arms, and plays with her knotted necklace. He can feel the energy of his people, this wigwam, the fire, and the stars. He knows something is about to happen. He does not know what it is, but he feels the thrill of his people and knows whatever is about to happen will be *special*.

The blanket over the doorway moves. The whispers of his people grow, and the fire swirls. Draped in a buckskin cape and tunic, the Storyteller's sister enters the wigwam. Her hair is long and white. It hangs loose over her shoulders. The older children clamor and nudge each other. *Look! It's Dancing Rain, the Grandmother Storyteller!* She floats across the room like a majestic eagle approaching its nest. She readies the people to hear the story. Dancing Rain points to the little children, and directs them to sit in the laps of their older siblings and cousins. The tiny hero of our story is invited to sit in front of one of his cousins. It makes him feel older to be sitting with the big children. That feeling of something exciting about to happen puts a smile on his face. He looks at his mother across the wigwam. She smiles back at him.

Dancing Rain speaks, reminding the older children to take care of the little ones. The older ones stop fidgeting to set a good example. The small ones see how straight and silently older children are sitting, and they do the same. Then Grandmother Dancing Rain leaves the wigwam.

From somewhere in the night, wolves howl, and a faint drumbeat accompanies their songs. The people are so quiet that the sounds of the burning logs capture everyone's attention. Just then, Dancing Rain returns. Her arms are filled with large bundles of kindling, a long stick, and four rolled-up hides.

She begins to dance. The soft sound of her moccasins touching the earth is the rhythm of a heartbeat, the fire dims until the light in the wigwam is very faint. Everyone can see Grandmother's dancing shadow circling the fire, and her burdens grow heavier…and…heavier in her arms. The distant drumming stops. The wind grows stronger. Now the little boy thinks he can hear the faint melody of a flute being carried in the wind.

Grandmother Dancing Rain speaks. "You have lived long, Great-Grand-father, your life is good. Would you do anything different if you could walk your life's path again?" Her voice is childlike—it *is* a child's voice! It lifts through the smokehole and up to the stars. It seems as though she speaks to the stars themselves.

"I would have carried a lighter burden," she answers in the deep, gentle voice of Great-Grandfather. Again, her voice, but *not* her voice. It comes from the corners of the wigwam. She drops the remaining bundles with a *thud*, and the wind and its music stops. The wigwam is dark and silent. Dancing Rain circles the fire again, adding the remaining handfuls of kin-dling as she dances.

As the fire rises and grows bright, the little boy is so fascinated with the dance, he doesn't notice that Little Hawk, the Storyteller, has entered and begins playing the hand drum. The sound startles the boy. Even his older cousin, Circling Eagle, who was also watching Dancing Rain, jumps. But Circling Eagle laughs, so the boy laughs, too. Sometimes it is fun to be star-tled. Little Hawk sings The Welcome Song with his hand drum, and the clan echoes the welcome, as Dancing Rain settles in front of her bundles near the fire. Then, for a time, the stories continue. Sometimes, they are so real and so startling, but if his *cousin* Circling Eagle doesn't act scared, why should *he* feel frightened?

Another story. The boy squirms with excitement. Mother has told him the same story many times, and the boy knows that it is an old, old story. Even though the story is an old one, the way the Storyteller tells it makes it come to life and makes it seem new. The People listen to the story and *become* the story, and the fire listens to the story and becomes the story as well. Even the sounds outside the wigwam become the story. The Story-teller's eyes shift, dance from face to face, lingering long enough to appre-ciate each person's reaction, like a hummingbird darting from flower to flower. The boy falls asleep in his cousin's lap dreaming big, colorful dreams.

For weeks after the storytelling, the boy pretends to be Little Hawk. He changes his voice and carries a drum. He watches the fire carefully. He be-comes so good at imitating Little Hawk that his older cousins laugh and ask him to repeat the performance for the *even bigger* boys and girls. He creeps up behind them, and with a loud drum beat, he makes them jump!

He does this so often that his people begin to call him Startle Drumming.

Startle Drumming, later known as Many Smiles, never forgot the visit of the Storyteller and he could summon a smile anytime he chose, just by remembering. Soon, because this is the way with the very young, Startle Drumming forgot the words of the stories Little Hawk told. All that remained were the feelings that magical night invoked. Most of us, if we find a quiet place, close our eyes, and travel through our memory, might be able to bring back the feeling of a loved one's bedtime stories or a song which still remains deep in our spirit, even if we do not recall all the words of the story or the melody of the song. Somewhere inside him, Startle Drumming *did* remember one story, the one that Dancing Rain danced to and whose words he could not understand, and yet, just as Dancing Rain had taught him by setting her heavy bundles down, for the rest of his life he always carried a lighter burden.

2.2 At the Village of Little Hawk and Dancing Rain: Beginning Formal Training as a Storyteller

(Please note: The story alluded to is the story of Grandmother Rock and First Child, an adaptation of the traditional Seneca tale of how stories came to be.)

Startle Drumming's Grandfather, Deer Cloud, took him on a long walk through the woods. Deer Cloud packed a sleeping bundle so Startle Drumming knew they would be going a long way. They crossed a stream, balancing themselves on the long, rough skin of a fallen cedar. They wove through the briars and the raspberry bushes. Startle Drumming's legs told the story in small cuts and scratches.

"Grandfather, I'd like to know where we are going."

"You'll see," said the grandfather.

They walked through the bog. Startle Drumming had to grab the generous arms of the swamp maple to stop himself from being pulled down by the mud of the bog. Grandfather knew his own footing and smiled as he watched his grandson learn how to cope with the pitfalls of the path.

"Grandfather, Grandfather," Startle Drumming said, "I'd like to know when we are going to arrive."

"When we get there," said Deer Cloud.

They reached a clearing of soft moss, and Grandfather Deer Cloud sent Startle Drumming to collect small sticks and kindling. Then he took his fire bow from his bag, and made a fire the way his grandfather had made a fire when he was even younger than Startle Drumming was now. Once they had made a fire, they spread their sleeping mats, and after they had eaten, they let the fire die so that they could see the stars. Startle Drumming rested his eyes for just a minute, but when he opened them again the Sun was rising, and Grandfather was bundling their belongings.

"Grandfather, Grandfather, Grandfather, I'd like to know if today will be as difficult as yesterday was."

"When the day is over, you will know for yourself," Deer Cloud smiled.

They walked the deer trails of the hot sands. The mosquitoes danced around them. The Sun shone so brightly that the boy walked with his eyes closed, opening them every five paces and then closing them again. When the Sun was overhead and all the animals were at their midday naps, Grandfather led his grandson to a stream. The smooth, wet stones at the bottom of the stream bed made Startle Drumming's feet want to dance for joy and gratitude. So the boy danced and thanked the stream and the rocks. Deer Cloud smiled, quietly giving thanks. Grandfather and Grandson drank the cold water, they bathed themselves, and rested in the beauty of the natural surroundings.

"Grandfather, Grandfather, I'd like to know if there are more cool streams further along that we can dance in, and drink from, and be grateful for, and soothe our feet, and bathe in, and lie down next to, hearing the stream sing its song of peace."

"For now, we have *this* stream and *its* song of peace. My Grandson, let us enjoy what we have *now*," Deer Cloud said.

After they rested, they walked along the stream bed, and the water was so clear that Startle Drumming could never tell if the waters ran deep or shallow. The slippery fallen logs in the stream played tricks on the boy, tripping him, then bouncing up and down with mischievous splash-laughter.

The river rocks danced under the boy's feet. In places, the current grew strong, pushing the boy, testing his balance.

"Grandfather, Grandfather, Grandfather…Grandfather?"

Deer Cloud lifted his finger to silence his grandson. He turned back and looked along the course of the stream. There, floating in the water, was a long, dark-brown, thick, perfect feather of a turkey vulture. The feather traveled quickly in the stream's current, heading straight for the young boy.

"Do you see it?" Deer Cloud asked.

Startle Drumming trailed his fingers into the water and the feather came straight for them. He removed the feather from the water, admired its beauty, and tucked the feather behind his ear. He spread his arms in gratitude for the wind that blew, the stream that carried the feather to his hand, to the river, and to the turkey vulture for giving such a gift.

Grandfather and Grandson noticed a path that intersected with the river. The path was wide and sandy. On one side, pine trees gave way to a moss-filled meadow. On the other, blueberries grew among the oak and pine. Deer Cloud and Startle Drumming walked toward a leaning maple tree that shaded the hot sands of the path. To the left, just beyond the maple, the boy saw a large wigwam rising like a hill in a clearing with a trail of silver-gray smoke rising from an opening at the top of the wigwam.

"Grandfather, are we here? I'd *really* like to know if we're here."

"We're always *here*. Yes, Grandson, yes. We have reached our destination."

They walked into the wigwam. Welcoming faces of cousins and smiles of old friends—the village greeted them. Just outside the wigwam, a wide log had been shaped into a cooking pot. The wooden pot was full of delicious soup, warmed by heated rocks from the fire, that were placed into the soup. A boy, a little older than Startle Drumming, offered a bowl of soup first to Grandfather, then to the grandson. They were led into the wigwam. A place was made for Startle Drumming between the cousins, and everyone waited.

Startle Drumming was seated with the children and Grandfather Deer Cloud sat with the elders, high in the wigwam, away from the door. A feeling of peaceful joy filled the wigwam, and outside the sound of a flute began its song. Blue jays and cicadas joined the flute and the wind whispered softly, *all is well*.

The door covering was drawn back. A man, about the same age as Grandfather, dressed in shells and feathers, in bone and quillwork, stepped into the wigwam. It was the Storyteller, Little Hawk!

Little Hawk walked slowly to the center of the wigwam, carrying his flute. His smiling eyes looked at every face. As soon as their eyes met, a great smile brightened Startle Drumming's face. When the man spoke, Startle Drumming just knew that Grandfather Little Hawk was speaking to *him*.

The boy listened and watched the Storyteller move and make signs with his hands as he told a story about the very first story, how that story had been told to a young child by Grandmother Rock—the ancestor of all rocks, stones, and pebbles—who knew the story of the time before time. As the boy listened, he forgot that he was sitting in a wigwam listening to a story. The storytelling was a bright light to him. It opened wide the imagination to the Storytellers, Warriors, Chiefs, and Puoins of long ago. The Sun in a story could rise and set in a second, could go backwards and forwards, leap generations into the past, jump into tomorrow, and return to the present in a single sentence.

As the great shadow of the ancient Storyteller shifted and danced, the boy felt he'd never wanted anything so much in all the world as to be that shadow, be that voice, and to hear the stories from the ancient rock.

Then it was over, and Little Hawk sat down next to his sister, Dancing Rain. The people brought gifts. The boy waited for the Storyteller to leave the wigwam and, when Little Hawk and Dancing Rain left, Startle Drumming followed them.

The two elders, the Storytellers, knelt by a tree and opened a basket. In the basket was a blanket. Then Little Hawk took off his feathers and shells and quills and rattles and placed them with respect and care in the blanket. Startle Drumming noticed how Grandfather Little Hawk and Grandmother Dancing Rain cleaned the flutes and packed them in another basket. Then the two of them wrapped the many gifts they received that day, and stood to leave, gathering their baskets.

The boy did not know what came over him to run and shout, "Storyteller, Storyteller, Storyteller!"

"Young man, young man, young man!" shouted the Storyteller. The boy stopped in his tracks and laughed. Storyteller laughed with him.

"I would like to know if I could be a Storyteller."

The Storyteller smiled. "I would like to know if I can be a child."

The boy smiled so wide that the Storyteller could see all of his teeth—even the brand-new, grown-up tooth pushing right in front.

"Storyteller, Storyteller, you can! I saw you. You were the boy on the rock in the story, and then you were the rock in the story. And then you were even the grandmother in the story! You were a turtle, and the tree, and... and...and...everything! So if you can be a child, can I be a Storyteller?"

"Young man, anyone who can be a child can be a Storyteller with the right work. Now, do you have a gift for us? Because it is as Grandmother Rock said, *'If you hear a story, it is good to bring a gift for the Storytellers.'*"

The boy smiled. He *did* have a gift. He reached behind his ear and produced the turkey vulture feather. He presented it to the Storytellers. Dancing Rain smiled. "This is a good feather for a Storyteller," she said to her brother, admiring the feather. She untied one of the bundles. She very carefully placed the turkey vulture feather in a special part of the bundle and put the bundle back in the basket.

The Storyteller reached for the narrow, leather strap that hung around his neck. Pulling it over his head, he took it off. Hanging from the strap was a small bag, old and worn. The leather was very soft as if the bag had been opened and closed more times than can be counted.

"This is my story heart," said Little Hawk. He emptied the bag into the boy's hand. A single gray stone rolled into the boy's small palm—just a plain, gray stone. It had become shiny from being handled so often.

"Now, who do you want to be?"

"Who? Storyteller, *who?* I said I wanted to be a St—"

"No, no, no! I mean do you want to be the bag or the stone?"

The boy smiled. "The stone."

So Startle Drumming and Little Hawk played. The stone became a cloud and the bag was a hunter. Then the bag was a long-armed spirit and the stone was a timid rabbit. Time passed, and the two played.

"Young man, young man, do you want to be a Storyteller?" the Storyteller Little Hawk asked.

The boy nodded.

"Then the first thing you must do is find your story heart. Put your fingers into the earth here, and think about Grandma Rock who told all the stories that existed before time. All rocks are part of her, so all rocks can tell a story. Put your fingers into the earth here, and dig until you find something."

The boy put his hand into the rich, forest soil. His fingers scraped and dug until they loosed a stone, not much bigger than a pebble. It was sharp-edged and shone like a wet river rock. The boy was pleased that this was going to be his new heart, his story heart.

"Now give it to me."

Startle Drumming did as he was asked. Smiling, Little Hawk handed the glittering pebble to Dancing Rain. She held it up to the light and nodded her approval.

"I name this stone Every Name," Grandmother Dancing Rain declared. "It is the child of Grandmother Rock, the knower of all stories. Tonight it will sleep with its brother stone, whose name is also Every Name."

She put Startle Drumming's stone into the same bag with Little Hawk's stone.

"Come back to me tomorrow, and I will give you your stone," Dancing Rain said.

Startle Drumming hurried back to the wigwam to find his grandfather, Deer Cloud, smoking by the fire with the other grandfathers. He knew not to interrupt the circle, so he closed his eyes and listened to the elders as they talked.

"Turtles," he thought, and he imagined the elders with shells on their backs, craning their long necks to take puffs of the pipe. He giggled to himself. When he was a great Storyteller, whenever he had to be a turtle, he would honor these elders by imitating them. Soon all talk was murmur, and the boy fell asleep.

In the morning, at dawn, the boy ran down to the river to have a swim and splash with the other children. An enormous flock of purple martins glided from point to point on the horizon and the boys pretended that the birds were stars that had forgotten where to hide during the day.

Then they dressed, cleaned the stack of bowls that had been left along-side the river, and ran off to serve the elders, which was a special honor for the boys and the girls of that village.

"Who serves Grandfather Little Hawk?" the boy asked.

One girl spoke up. "He's my father's uncle. I serve Grandfather Little Hawk!" She said it with honor. The child's name was Playful Otter. "My brother serves my grandmother, Dancing Rain, who is also a Storyteller. My parents are Howling Wolf and Gray Dog, the Puoins of the tribe. They make sure this village and all its people's lives are filled with good medicine."

After the boy had given his grandfather the steaming bowl of sweet and delicious chufa nut and fish soup, he ate two bowlfuls with rich, dark, acorn ashcakes. Dancing Rain appeared with a small, leather pouch that she had made the night before. The pouch hung from a leather strap, like a medicine bag.

"In this pouch is your story heart," she explained. "It is a source of wisdom. You must wake it now and let it breathe while you're still young because only a child can wake the story heart. But to keep it awake and beating, every day, no matter what, before you lay on your mat to go to sleep, you must open this bag and let the stone look around. Otherwise, the stone may fall silent forever and cease to tell you stories. If you forget to play with the stone even for a day, find a child younger than you to play with it because only through the play and joy of childlike laughter can a story live in the hearts of others."

She turned and nodded to Grandfather, then crouched down and looked Startle Drumming in the eye. "Little Hawk sat with your grandfather last night. You were asleep. All shared the pipe and it was good. We spoke and we agreed. On the day the last of your milk teeth has wiggled out of your mouth, if you have kept the stone alive, and if you've played with it every day, then return, and you will learn our way of storytelling."

Grandmother Dancing Rain gave the pouch to Deer Cloud, and Grandfather Deer Cloud admired the woman's sewing. Then he passed the stone to his Startle Drumming. The boy took the gift in his hands and opened it. The bag was only big enough for two pebbles, a little wider and about as long as the boy's thumb. He turned the bag upside down and let the beautiful stone he'd found the night before tumble into his hand.

That night, Little Hawk's stone stayed up until the dawn reminding Startle Drumming's stone of every story that had ever happened since the beginning of time, which was also the beginning of stories. That old stone, when it had started beating, spent the night with the stone of Little Hawk's long-ago teacher. *That* stone had heard stories from *another* stone stretching back, back, back to that first child on the first rock who heard the first story. Grandmother Dancing Rain put the bag around the boy's neck, where it remained, when it wasn't being played with, or at risk of getting wet, for the rest of Startle Drumming's days.

Those of you who hear the story and wish to become Storytellers, find a pebble, put it in a pouch, and hold, touch, and play with it every day. Don't simply choose the first rock you see. Look for the one that chooses *you*, the one that says to you, "I'm the one for you." Storytelling comes from nature. It, like you, is a part of nature. Draw upon nature as a source. Storytelling has a history of fun and play as it teaches. It is as old as the imagination itself, and as young as laughter. Stories teach us to live in a good way, and to keep play in our daily lives is a very good way to live indeed.

And we are not the only creatures who tell stories. The bees dance their stories so their sisters may live in a good way, the whales sing to each other so that they may live in a good way, the ants and the wolves have their own means of communicating stories to each other, which helps each of these creatures to live in a good way.

Take your time to master play. Take Grandmother Dancing Rain's advice seriously. You must strive to play every day to keep strong your storytelling heart.

2.3 My Sister, the Eagle—My Brother, the Rabbit: Learning Empathy for All Life to Prepare for Call and Response

A year went by, and the boy played with his pebble and with the leather pouch. Sometimes he felt uninspired and his imagination lost its ability to transform that stone into a bird, or a warrior, or a boulder, but not usually. Telling a child to play is like telling a fish to swim.

The tribe noticed that this was a very observant boy. Within the year, his mother's brother, Becomes Unseen, was teaching him to stalk and to hunt. In a few years, Startle Drumming became an excellent hunter, catching small game close to camp to bring to the cooking pot. Each time he hunted, he felt joy for bringing food to his people, and sorrow for taking a plant or an animal's life. To show respect for the creatures that he hunted, he kept a small part of each of those creatures and kept them in a blanket as a reminder that they feed his people.

Often, he would play with his stone, and he would take one of these items from the blanket and tell a story he had learned from the tracks of the rabbit, or the flight of the crow. He spoke to Painted Sky, the Puoin, who knew the healing ways of the body and the spirit, and she told him that if he kept calling to the ancestors for wisdom, someday they would teach him how to hunt not only to satisfy his physical hunger, but to satisfy his spiritual hunger as well.

And so it was. One day the ancestors responded.

That day, Startle Drumming returned to the village carrying an eagle and a rabbit. He had already wiped away his tears when he approached his grandfather. "Please Grandfather, I wish to speak with you, my Uncle, Becomes Unseen, and the Puoin, Painted Sky, who knows the ways of the spirit."

When the boy sat in front of the elders, he said, "Today, I—I followed a rabbit run through the tall plants in the field. At the end of the rabbit run, I noticed fresh droppings. Uncle told me this is a good way to tell how old a track is."

"It is as the boy says. I taught him in just that way," Becomes Unseen replied.

As he continued his story, Startle Drumming found himself acting out what he was saying, squatting just as he did as he had tracked that afternoon. "Just beyond the ferns was a sandy clearing. I could tell by the round mark in the sand that the rabbit had rested here. See?" He drew a mark in the ashes of the fire pit, and the elders nodded. "The rabbit was big. You can see him here. His tracks said he had hopped one step further, and had craned his neck upward. Rabbit must have been afraid of Sister Eagle. I could read in the sand how hungry Sister Eagle had been. She had swooped silently down, reaching out her talons, and had snatched Rabbit by the brown fur on his back."

The boy was on his feet, soaring, swooping, and grabbing at his uncle's neck. "Sister Eagle had taken off straight ahead, in the direction of the tall trees. I could tell because both wings swept the ground evenly toward the big oak tree. But, of course, once the eagle took to the sky, the track ended. You see, this rabbit was enormous, and heavy for a rabbit. Sister Eagle had swept the ground with her wings many times before climbing into the air. The track was fresh." The last fact he whispered, as if it was a secret he wanted to keep from the rabbit and the eagle.

"I can't explain, but in my mind I could see Sister Eagle fighting to gain height despite the weight of the rabbit. I walked in the direction of the trees. There, on the ground by the white oak, lay the rabbit. Why had Sister Eagle abandoned her meal? What in the sky could have challenged her? Why did she leave this rabbit motionless on the ground? I picked up the rabbit and started to walk back home. I am a big boy. I already have eight of my grownup teeth. But for all the years I've lived, I can't imagine what would make this feared hunter surrender her dinner."

The boy stood up and continued his story. "The wind picked up and made the small plants dance." The boy danced like the small plants. "Something told me that to understand the story of the eagle I had to see through the eyes of an eagle. So I ran to the oak tree. *Oak Tree, Oak Tree, Oak Tree, I have decided to climb you.* I told the oak tree. *Please hold my rabbit in your branches. I want to see with the eyes of an eagle.* And that's just what I did, I put the rabbit right in the branches of the oak tree."

Startle Drumming looked at the elders. "Sometimes the older boys and girls make jokes because of my fear of falling. Climbing a tree is easy at first, and when you're focused on the branches, and reaching upwards, and thinking about things like eagles and dropped rabbits, very quickly you climb higher than you realize. When you look down, you're scared.

"That is what happened to me. I imagined myself falling, crashing to the ground like the rabbit, to become food for the crows. I caught my breath, and felt trapped in the branches. And then I thought, *this is what the rabbit must have felt!* I could almost feel *both* our hearts racing. I had shared the feeling with the rabbit, so now I could share that feeling with you, with anyone!

"I could bring not only the meat of the rabbit, but the story of the rabbit back to my people and help everyone understand how the rabbit felt while it was so high in the air—held by a hungry eagle. Then I thought of myself in the tree, and how high I had climbed, and how difficult it was going to be to get back down. Part of me was frightened, but another part of me soared above my body just like an eagle. I imagined myself years from now, remembering, telling the story of when I was a boy and how I had gotten caught in a tree, and how it had taught me to see through the rabbit's eyes, and the eagle's eyes. And now here I am."

The Pouin, Painted Sky, spoke, "This is good, Startle Drumming," she said. "You are telling your elders what happened to that eagle and this rabbit. It's a fine rabbit, very plump and very big."

"Grandmother Puoin, that must mean *every* rabbit has a story!" Startle Drumming exclaimed. "But I will continue to tell this rabbit's story. I am in the tree, feeling the fear the rabbit must have felt. I wanted to remember the feeling, so I could share it when I told the story of the rabbit. Then I looked down. I could see my village, the stream, a hillside, and beyond that, the forest. I remembered the colors and the silence high in the tree. I made myself remember how the high wind sang differently than it did on the ground, And all of a sudden, I could see through the eyes of the flying eagle. So I spoke in eagle language.

"Sister Eagle, why did you drop the rabbit? I asked.

"Then I saw my answer. In a little heap, not too far from the rabbit, lay Sister Eagle, who had taken her last breath."

Startle Drumming frowned and continued his story. "I hurried down the oak tree like an oversized squirrel. I grabbed the rabbit and ran so fast I felt that I was flying across the field. I knelt beside Sister Eagle. Could Sister Eagle's day of quiet come right in the middle of a hunt? This is my question. This is what I do not understand. I've seen animals hunt, and I've hunted myself, but—but can the time of quiet come as it came to Sister Eagle?"

The boy reached toward the golden feathers of the eagle and stroked them reverently. He felt sad for the beautiful eagle. "I never knew that the time to join the ancestors could *just come* so quickly. What is it that hunts a hunter?"

Deer Cloud put his hand lovingly on his grandson's head. "Do not let it trouble you to learn we can join the ancestors at anytime."

"But I also felt that if I told the story of this eagle and this rabbit to you, some of what they were would remain not only in the stomachs of my people, but also in their hearts. Finally, I carried back the eagle and the rabbit. I don't know if I carried them properly. I took the eagle in one hand, and the rabbit in the other. Will the spirit of the eagle be angry that I kept them separate?"

"The eagle knows the rabbit is heavy, my son," the Puoin answered.

Later, when they were called to supper, the children heard the story of the eagle and the rabbit. The boy told the story as if it were an old legend, and then at the end, Startle Drumming surprised everyone by revealing that *he* was the boy and the very stew they were eating now contained that wonderful rabbit that had been hunted and dropped by Sister Eagle. The children were delighted, and they agreed that the stew was sweeter because they knew the story of the animal that had fed them. Somehow, by being nourished by the lesson of the story and by the food itself, it was as if they had eaten twice.

That night, though he carefully wrapped a piece of rabbit fur and two eagle feathers into his blanket, Startle Drumming forgot to play with his pebble.

2.4 Startle Drumming Makes a Trade with the Sky: Knowing Your Listeners and Your Purpose

One night, Startle Drumming felt a wiggle in his ninth tooth. That night, a heavy storm approached from the warm land of the south. The storm shook the wigwam with its mighty thunder. The little ones were so frightened that they cried.

Startle Drumming had noticed that all children, skunk children, raccoon children, even puppies, all feared the thunder and flashes of a storm. Once, he'd witnessed a skunk kitten lifting its tail to threaten a flash of lightning, and then turn in confusion when a flash appeared elsewhere, and finally, trembling at the storm, he had curled into a ball, close to his mother and sisters.

Startle Drumming's great-grandmother, Two Heartbeat, was the Clan Mother, the oldest person in the tribe. By village tradition, she approved the selection of a chief, and the village council often asked for her opinion on important matters. She sat and slept "high" in the wigwam, furthest from the door in the place of honor, near the Elm Post. High on the post above her, hung the ceremonial drum. Startle Drumming had never played the ceremonial drum, had never even touched it or the Elm Post. That right was reserved for the elders. But he had heard the drum many times. Its skin was of moose hide, and it was large as the Full Moon, and its sound was the loudest of heartbeats. When seven elders drummed on it in unison, it was like listening to all hearts beating as one.

With the storm crashing and flashing outside the wigwam, all the very little ones were frightened as he himself had been when he was small. The children asked Great-Grandmother Two Heartbeat to tell the story about Little Thunder. She smiled, and because her eyes had smiled so often, happiness had worn foot paths across her cheeks and towards her ears. In fact, her smile had made footpaths to and from her eyes and ears and nose and mouth as if happy ideas had run like deer along the outside of her face shouting, *See how good! Hear how good! Taste how good! Smell how good!* As if every sense wanted to share that happiness with the others. And those feelings of happiness had worn deep furrows to make their trip swift and easy. Startle Drumming hoped that when he was an elder, the footpaths across his face would be lines of happiness.

Startle Drumming had never heard Great-Grandmother Two Heartbeat tell the story, usually the story was told by his aunt or grandmother. The wigwam was dark, and mother and uncle were sleeping. Grandfather was also sleeping far from the door. Since Startle Drumming was still a child, he slept close to the door, and one of his important jobs was to make sure that the very little ones were safe and comfortable, and did not wander alone outside the wigwam at night.

"My children," Great-Grandmother Two Heartbeat said, "come to the high post and sit in front of me by the fire, my little ones."

Immediately, the crying stopped. The little ones smiled. Great-Grandmother moved back toward the wall of the wigwam, until her sleeping palette was against the Elm Post. "When Becomes Unseen brings me the children's sleeping mats, I wish to put my hand on his cheek and smile at him, because I remember when he was a little one and lay in front of my Aunt Red Branch and heard the same story of Little Thunder. Red Branch was Clan Mother then. Now her sleeping mat is spread in the Wigwam of the Ancestors. But she gave me this story, and even longer ago, she named me Two Heartbeat. I remember the night Red Branch named you, Becomes Unseen. My child, you are a man, but can you remember what it felt like to lie in front of the fire, and listen to the stories of the grandmother?"

Becomes Unseen laughed, spread the mats, and knelt near Great-Grandmother, respectfully positioning himself so that he did not block her view of the fire. The children, even though they were very young, remembered to crawl behind their elders, near the walls of the wigwam, because children must not be between the fire and an adult, except when the adults invited them to be there.

"The boy near the door who hunts for stories—let him tend the fire tonight. Do you know why, little ones?"

"We will know why when Great-Grandmother tells us," came a little voice.

"Because tonight the sky is named Startle Drumming!"

Just then, as if in agreement, the lightning flashed and the thunder boomed, and everyone jumped. As the children cried, Startle Drumming remembered how his cousin encouraged him to feel brave all those years ago at that storytelling when he wanted to cry with fear. He resolved to defeat the little ones' fears with laughter.

"Sky!" he said loud enough for the little ones to hear. "You're not Startle Drumming, I am! Why have you taken my name?"

The children laughed.

"Sky has good ears," Startle Drumming said. "But, little ones, the next time you hear the thunder, please ask the sky to give me back my name." This delighted the children. They couldn't wait for the next startling drumbeat so they could ask the sky to return their cousin's name to him. In this way, Startle Drumming helped the little ones forget their fears.

"Good, very good, what you say, Boy Without a Name." Boy Without a Name (Startle Drumming) had already turned to gather the kindling for the fire, but he heard the tone of approval in Clan Mother's voice. In that moment, listening to her voice, he could imagine her smile. He thought, *We are happy. We are doing good work.* And in his mind's eye, he could see those footpaths of happiness worn from Great-Grandmother's eyes to her ears to her mouth. He felt those smile lines stretch all the way across the wigwam to his ears, his eyes, his mouth. Those deep, furrowed paths were leading the little children to a place of happiness.

Once again, the thunder boomed. This time, the little ones laughed and said, "Sky, please give our cousin back his name!"

The Boy Whose Name Had Been Taken By the Sky (Startle Drumming) built up the fire. As he worked on the fire, he spoke to the sky so that the little ones and Great-Grandmother could hear him. "You may keep my name, Sky. I will trade it for the many smiles of Our People."

"What do you think little ones? Do you think your cousin has made a good trade with the sky?" Great-Grandmother asked. "Do you agree to the trade? Now, when the thunder startles you, you will smile and laugh at yourselves. This boy has given his name to the sky so you children won't cry anymore. So from now on, when you talk about Startle Drumming, you will be talking about the stormy sky, and when you talk to your cousin you will call him Many Smiles."

The boy felt so happy that his throat grew tight. He had been given a new name! He'd been given a strong name that would help him find his place in the world. Aftere he made sure the fire was correct, he excused himself and walked outside into the rain.

The little ones wondered why he was leaving the wigwam, but Great-Grandmother guessed, and she approved. The boy opened his small leather pouch and held his storytelling heart, his playmate—that pebble—in his hand. He whispered to it, "Remember this story of my naming, my friend. Keep it and tell it to the other rocks, stones, and pebbles, because this is a good day."

His long hair and bare shoulders were drenched with rain as he placed the stone back into the pouch. Then he turned his eyes to the storm. Inside, warm and dry, the children prepared to hear Great-Grandmother's story about Little Thunder. Once again, the lightning flashed and the thunder roared, and after the thunder, the little ones could hear a boy's voice, shouting to the storm, "Do you hear, sky? It's a trade! From now on, you're Startle Drumming, and I'm Many Smiles!"

Everyone who heard him…smiled.

2.5 *Little Thunder's Wedding:*
Learning a Formal Story
and Playing with the Plot

(This is an adaptation of a traditional Mi'kmaw story.)

This is the story Great-Grandmother Two Heartbeat told of Little Thunder's marriage.

Many generations ago this story was born. This story was born from truth and nature, and it fit Our People like the finest buckskin.

Listen, my little ones and travel with me in your imagination to a place where there are no brothers and no cousins, just one very small wigwam. Our friend Little Thunder had his parents, and the beaver, the eagles, the turtles, the seagulls, and the skunk to keep him company. Little Thunder was especially close to a skunk family that lived near the wigwam. Like Little Thunder, the skunk-child, whose name was Open Paths, was all alone except for her parents, and the swift deer, and the playful wind, and Little Thunder, the Two-Legged, to keep her company. So they played together and ate together and grew up friends. Because the skunk and Little Thunder had grown up together, and because Little Thunder had never seen any other human besides his parents, and because the skunk had never seen any skunk except her own parents, Little Thunder and the skunk imagined that one day they would...

Would *what?* Everyone wondered. Great-Grandmother Two Heartbeat paused, until everyone listening couldn't wait to hear. Her eyes twinkled.

...marry each other!

Everyone laughed.

Aho! So you agree with Little Thunder's parents, I see. Little Thunder's parents were friends with Open Path's parents, and both sets of parents agreed to send their children out into the world to find suitable mates because they could not imagine that a marriage between skunks and Two-Leggeds could ever work. So Open Path's parents asked their daughter to go to the forest along the coast to find a mate for herself. The boy, now a young man, likewise was advised by his parents to find a mate for himself among the women of Chief Shakes the Earth's village.

Some of the children were still giggling about the idea of marrying a skunk.

I can hear you, my children, laughing, imagining what life would be like if you were friends with skunks! But the truth is that Our People and the skunks have been friends for a long, long time. Our relationship to skunks is much like the relationships we have with our own brothers and sisters. If we respect each other, we do not have conflict, and when we don't respect each other, life immediately gets very unpleasant for everyone involved because, you know, not even the skunk likes its own spray.

I believe that the boy and the skunk were not wrong to imagine that they would be very happy together. Still both the boy and the skunk were obedient children who trusted the wisdom of their parents and agreed to go out into the world to find suitable mates. A girl human for the boy human, she held up two fingers on either hand and made them walk towards each other, *and a boy skunk for the girl skunk.* She held up her right fist, and raised her little finger to imitate the body and tail of a skunk and she smelled the little finger and made a face. Her expression showed that this skunk smelled very strong. All the children laughed.

The boy and the skunk had agreed to travel together to the wigwam of Glooscap. Like every one of Our People, Little Thunder and the skunk, Open Paths, knew that they could count on Glooscap to help them on their journey. Little Thunder knew that Open Paths was a creature of the night and respected her ways, and Open Paths knew that Little Thunder was a creature of daylight and respected his ways. Thus they only traveled at dawn and dusk. By day, Little Thunder watched over his friend and hunted and gathered. When Little Thunder slept, Open Paths watched over her friend and hunted and gathered. Their travels together were full of laughter and wonder and they grew to trust each other completely.

As Great-Grandmother Two Heartbeat spoke, her arms moved. When she spoke about the sleeping skunk, she made her arm flow out and wrap around her head to imitate the sleeping skunk. When she spoke about the pair hunting and traveling, she showed the children with her fists and fingers how the two friends walked together.

Finally, as day was becoming night on the seventh day of their journey, Little Thunder looked out into the bay and saw an island.

"Look out there in the bay—that's Glooscap's Island!" he exclaimed. "Hop on my back, my friend, and I will swim us out to the island." Open Paths agreed.

When they reached Glooscap's Island, the two friends walked up to the cooking fire where First Grandmother, Nukumi, was preparing a meal. Open Paths and Little Thunder felt as if they had seen Nukumi before, perhaps in dreams they had enjoyed while they were still in their mother's womb. Nukumi was the woman who had taken care of them before they'd been born.

"Go right in, my dears, the food will be ready soon," Grandmother Nukumi said. She pointed to the wigwam, which was very large and beautifully made from bark of elm and birch.

Inside, at the Elm Post, in a seat of honor, sat not Glooscap, but his friend Abistanaooch, which is a sort of weasel, who was the first friend in the world, and is the inventor of friendship. Glooscap sat in the second place of honor, next to his friend. Open Paths and Little Thunder immediately felt at home, and were invited to sit high in the wigwam, even though they were very young for that honor.

When the two travelers had explained to Glooscap and to Abistanaooch that their parents had advised them to find mates, Glooscap agreed to help both of them. He invited them to stay for dinner and spend the night.

What a meal it was! My children, I want you to imagine drinking a stew from an acorn cap. Little Thunder and even Open Paths never imagined that such a tiny amount of stew could ever satisfy the hunger of either one of them. Our two friends were very disappointed they'd received so little food, but they did not want to be rude. They sipped their stew very slowly, enjoying the rich, dark taste of acorns and mushrooms, the strong taste of meat, and the sweetness of fruit and other strange but wonderful tastes neither had ever tried before. When they commented on how good the stew was, Grandmother Nukumi told the two friends that those acorn caps came from the seeds of the first oak and were the first acorn caps. Little Thunder noticed that no matter how many times he emptied the stew from the acorn cap, the same amount of stew remained.

Grandmother Nukumi explained that it was friendship that kept the bowls filled. "There is food for the body, and food for the spirit. Just as stew can fill the stomach, goodness to each other eases the hunger of the spirit." *Little Thunder and Open Paths could eat until they both felt very full, and very sleepy, and very welcome.*

During the night, Open Paths laid her head at Glooscap's feet, and Little Thunder laid his head at Open Path's feet. The wigwam was cold, but Abistanaooch gave Little Thunder a magical, black-fur blanket which Little Thunder could make grow out of his body whenever he needed a warm coat, so he could have fur just like a bear or a skunk.

Open Paths had never slept inside a wigwam before and wasn't used to sleeping at night. This caused her to have a bad dream, and in her sleep, she had sprayed. She was so sorry she'd caused a strong smell. Glooscap took her to the water to wash and gave her a clean, new cloak, made of thin hide that could grow from her body whenever she was feeling too hot or needed to wash. It was a hairless coat just like the skin of a Two-Legged. He also gave her a special comb.

When she used it, the comb made her hair grow long and silky and black. Glooscap warned her only to run the comb through her hair seven times, but when she saw herself reflected in the stream, and saw how beautiful she looked, she became vain and ran the comb through her hair twice more. Immediately, she saw two white streaks appear in her hair just where she had combed too much. A big tear rolled down Open Path's cheek. She realized her vanity had caused the streaks. She cried and whimpered, but her streaks never went away and whenever she saw her reflection in the water, she remembered humility is better than vanity.

Glooscap was very generous and liked the skunk very much. So he also gave her a special flute that she could use to sing and talk like a human. She raised the flute to her mouth and began to play.

She played the flute so beautifully, that Glooscap decided she needed a drumbeat with her music. He borrowed a hide from a great moose that lived in the clouds. With this hide, Glooscap made a drum for Little Thunder. Glooscap warned Little Thunder, "Be careful not to beat your drum so loudly that the clouds hear because, if they do, they will bring their hearth fires to the ground and dance on the earth."

When the dawn came, Open Paths said, "It is time to go on our way. Thank you, Glooscap, Abistanaoooch, and Nukumi."

"You may borrow my canoe if you promise to return it," *Glooscap said.* "I have made many canoes, and each time I lend one out, someone has forgotten to return it."

Little Thunder and Open Paths promised that they would return the canoe, but when they went to the place where Glooscap told them the canoe was, all they saw was a small island. They looked back toward Glooscap, but he was nowhere to be seen.

The small island lay between Glooscap's Island and the mainland, so Open Paths and Little Thunder swam to that small island and rested there.

"I wish we were back on the mainland," *said Open Paths.* "That way you would not have to carry me."

No sooner had the words escaped her mouth, but the island floated toward the mainland.

"We're moving! We're moving!" *Little Thunder shouted in disbelief.* "Look, Open Paths, this isn't an island, it's actually a canoe made out of stone and earth!"

As the canoe drifted closer to the mainland, the two friends realized that it was time to part company.

"You know I have to travel the streams to Chief Shakes the Earth's village, and you have to continue up the northern coast to reach the Great Forest," *Little Thunder sighed.* "Open Paths, I will miss you."

"I have never spent a day away from you, Little Thunder. I know I will miss your company too," *Open Paths said sadly.*

Just then, the magical canoe-island split in two. Part of it flowed up the coast toward the Great Forest, carrying Open Paths. Little Thunder's portion of the canoe squeezed and changed shape so it could fit in the narrow streams, and then traveled until it reached the fires of Chief Shakes the Earth's village.

Of course, Shakes the Earth's whole tribe was very interested in this young traveler who floated on a stone canoe. Shakes the Earth was a wise chief and he now considered what was best for The People. Now was not the time to say what he was thinking: "A strong warrior doesn't need magic. Just a good paddle and a well-built canoe. That is more than all this show."

Little Thunder had never seen other people before. He was amazed at how many different types there were, old ones, young ones, males, and females. Still, Little Thunder had no desire to marry any of them. "Maybe," *he thought,* "there are no women here I can marry."

However, this was not the case. Chief Shakes the Earth had a daughter, Mountain Flower, who had reached the age of marriage. Little Thunder wanted to please his parents, and he thought that meant he had to court this woman, and prove his worth to Shakes the Earth.

No one taught Little Thunder what he must do to court a woman. Little Thunder imagined he could capture any woman's heart by performing dazzling feats. So, he placed himself in front of her and his future father-in-law and announced to the whole tribe, "I am Little Thunder, and I am here to prove I am worthy to marry Mountain Flower!"

Shakes the Earth loved his daughter very much. She reminded him of his dear wife, who had left to tend the fires of the Cloud Nation a long time ago when their daughter was born. Now, even she took some time from her duties among the clouds to watch this young man try and win her daughter's hand.

"To prove my bravery and worthiness, and to win your heart, Mountain Flower, I will slide down the ice-capped mountain on a toboggan," *Little Thunder announced.*

"This boy is very, very, very foolish," *muttered the Chief.* "He doesn't know how dangerous it is to sled down that mountain. Still, he will climb the mountain, see the danger, and give up his impossible quest."

Open Paths, meanwhile, could find no companion in the Great Forest, at least one she cared to be with as much as she cared to be with Little Thunder. She asked her stone canoe to travel until she found her friend again. The canoe found Little Thunder just as he was declaring his intent to toboggan down the dangerous mountain. Open Paths hid in a pile of kindling and wondered what she could do to stop Little Thunder from killing himself because, even after he saw the steep cliffs and dangerous rocks of the ice-capped mountain, Little Thunder had been taught to do what he said he was going to do, which is sometimes wise, and sometimes very foolish.

So Little Thunder climbed the mountain, followed by several curious (and concerned) members of Chief Shakes the Earth's village. Open Path's heartbeat quickened and her breath grew rapid. She ran until she found Eagle sitting on a fallen tree. Open Paths startled him.

"Eagle, Eagle please help my friend, Little Thunder. If he is in danger, would you swoop down, pick him up, and bring him to safety?"

"You are my friend, Skunk. I feel happy to do this for you. May I also ask a favor of you?"

"Whatever you wish, Eagle."

"Then please tell me how you make your hair so black and soft."

"It's this wonderful comb Glooscap gave me. I'll gladly lend it to you. Use it only seven times, and your feathers will be black and silky and shine like my hair."

Eagle borrowed the comb and combed his body feathers until they were shiny and black. But he forgot to comb his head. By the time he remembered, he had already used the comb seven times, but he was so pleased with the result he forgot to count. So when he combed his head, with an eight, ninth, and tenth stroke, all his head feathers whitened like a mountaintop after a snowstorm. Eagle was not displeased. He thought this made him look...wise. However, Glooscap was not pleased. Eagle had not followed directions and without direction, an eagle would have to circle bigger and bigger and fly higher and higher before he could find his way home. That very day, Glooscap named him Circling Eagle. From that time on, whenever we say Circling Eagle's name, we always remember that a wise eagle must follow directions.

The children all laughed and pointed at their older cousin named Circling Eagle, who was happy to be included in the story. He pretended to comb his hair with his fingers. Great-Grandmother Two Heartbeat continued the story:

Little Thunder's toboggan flew off a cliff. Because they turned their heads and clenched their teeth and covered their eyes in horror, waiting for the sound of a toboggan crashing against the stones below, no one who had come along saw a swiftly swooping eagle coming out of the Sun across the high rock face. Circling Eagle dove skillfully, caught Little Thunder, and gently placed him at the foot of the mountain.

The children cheered, and cousin Circling Eagle flapped his arms as if they were wings, and lowered his brow to make his eyes look like an eagle's.

When Little Thunder shouted and waved from the foot of the mountain, those who had accompanied him imagined he had survived the great fall, and thought that this stranger must be very powerful indeed. But the Chief would not let him marry his daughter.

"All this proves is that you can fall from great heights and feel nothing. If this is true, then how are you going to be able to console my daughter when she is hurt?"

"My future wife and father-in-law! I can prove myself worthy of your family! I can run faster than anyone in this tribe in a foot race. Surely this would impress you, father-in-law to be, and you, my future bride."

"Well, he doesn't give up," *thought Mountain Flower.*

Open Paths thought fast. "How can I help him win?" *She went to talk to the wind.*

Wind did a round dance of joy when it saw Open Paths. "Skunk, you and I are friends. I know your parents well. They have called on me many times to clear the air after danger was past. There is no time when people are happier to feel me blow than after your family has used its power to stay safe.

What can I do for you now?"

Skunk explained that Little Thunder had to win a footrace in order to marry Shakes the Earth's daughter. "For you, Skunk, I will lift your friend and carry him swiftly to the finish line. I only ask that you let me try your flute. I would really like to play a tune."

"Of course," *said Open Paths.*

Because this was a magic flute, the wind made it sound like a person singing. Many people of Chief Shakes the Earth's village listened and learned the songs. The wind carried its magic music all over the land and that is how the magic flute got its name, Brother of the Wind. To this day, The People still sing the songs of Brother of the Wind.

Then the race began. The Chief's swiftest runners could not keep up with Little Thunder. Wind blew Little Thunder so that his body flew across the field and tore a hole in the side of the Chief's wigwam. Little Thunder spent the rest of the day patching the wigwam of his future father-in-law, with many apologies.

"This will never do," *grumbled the Chief.* "This boy runs so fast that he causes wigwams to be damaged. Every time he runs, my daughter will have to rebuild the wigwam."

"All this proves is that you can run away very quickly when danger is near," *said the Chief.* "If this is true, then how can I expect you to stand beside my daughter in times of trouble? She could not run as fast as you."

Little Thunder persisted. "Let me dance for you. I can dance and drum until the clouds come to the earth and dance on one million wet feet." *Little Thunder started to drum. The sound of his drumming shook the Earth and reached the Cloud Nation. The clouds loved the drumming and brought their rain to the earth. They also brought their fires of lightning with them, and their fires came close to burning the Chief's wigwam.*

"Enough!" *Shakes the Earth said firmly.* "This destructive behavior must stop—now!"

The drums were so loud and the rain splashed so hard against the ground that no one could hear him. But the Chief was wise and clever, so he decided on a plan. Shakes the Earth began to dance, harder and harder, until the earth shook, and the rocky ground that had been prepared for the dance split and cracked under his feet. Only then did he stop his dance. He smiled, "Please forgive me for ruining the dance. I guess I didn't know how heavy I really was."

The clouds then returned to the sky. Meanwhile, Wind and Circling Eagle visited Chief Shakes the Earth and explained that Little Thunder was showing respect for his parents' wishes that he marry, and how the skunk, Open Paths, was helping him.

"Maybe we can make a bargain," *Circling Eagle said.* "Open Paths is our friend. Little Thunder is our friend."

"We would like to see them happy," *Wind added.*

So Shakes the Earth, Wind, and Circling Eagle traveled together to visit Glooscap.

Glooscap invited his guests to feast just as he had invited Skunk and Little Thunder. After dinner, Glooscap looked at his friend Abistanaooch.

"These two friends are very different." *said Glooscap.* "One is a skunk, one is a human. But I am also different from my best friend. Friends do not have to be the same. A woman and a man should be happy to be different in many ways, but above all they should be friends. They should take care of each other, they should obey their parents, and help their people. Open Paths has helped Little Thunder, and Little Thunder and Open Paths are very good friends. We must arrange for them to be together."

Glooscap continued, "Here are two arrows I have created to help both our friends, not to hurt either of them. Chief, when you return to your village, send Little Thunder and your daughter to return my canoe on their way to his home to be married. When they pass the bluffs on the mainland near my home, I will lure the skunk to the edge of the bluffs. Then, let your daughter fire one arrow at Skunk. This will make Skunk's body sleep for half a year, and her spirit will be free to be human for half a year. Here is the other arrow, which your daughter must fire at Little Thunder. When it strikes him, his body will sleep for half the year, and his spirit will be free to be a skunk for the other half. In this way, the two friends can marry and they will live happily together, half the time as skunks, half the time as humans."

Glooscap handed two arrows to Chief Shakes the Earth. These arrows glowed with warm flames and would have singed the hands of anyone who held them, but Glooscap had created the arrows so, even though they blazed with fire, anyone could pick them up.

Chief Shakes the Earth thought Glooscap's plan was a reasonable idea. He returned home to his daughter and told her about it. Mountain Flower told her father she would go along with the plan. That day, she accepted Little Thunder's marriage proposal. Little Thunder felt relieved, but he did not feel happy. In fact, his heart was heavy.

Together, he and his bride-to-be stepped onto the canoe to head back toward Glooscap's Island and return the canoe to him. Little Thunder fell into a deep sleep just as the canoe headed away from Shakes the Earth's village. When the canoe came into view of the bluffs near Glooscap's Island, Mountain Flower saw the skunk on the bluff. She took an arrow and pulled back on the bowstring, but she just didn't have the heart to pierce the body of such a beautiful animal. Even though she understood the whole plan, her fingers could not release the arrow. She began to weep, fearing that now she would have to travel to Little Thunder's home and marry him.

Her mother's spirit happened to be tending the fire of the Cloud Nation close to the bluffs that day. She heard her daughter's cry and whispered to the girl, "My good daughter, I will do this thing for you." *She took Glooscap's arrows, and shot one at Open Paths and one at Little Thunder. Immediately, they both became skunks—that is to say, Little Thunder became a skunk, and Open Paths remained her true self.*

Overjoyed, Little Thunder the Skunk returned Mountain Flower to her village. Shakes the Earth's village held a marriage celebration for the two skunks, and invited Wind and Circling Eagle to celebrate with them. Then the two skunks returned the canoe to Glooscap and traveled home together. When the summer months came, and when thin hides make the best regalia, the pair turned into human beings. They had another wedding ceremony as humans, celebrating with their skunk and human parents. Glooscap, Nukumi, and Abistanaooch were invited. When the weather got cold, the pair turned to skunks again, found a warm burrow, and lived happily to old age together.

"Now my story is finished, my children, and the storm has passed," Great-Grandmother said.

By this time, the children were all asleep. Many Smiles crept along the floor and put his head on Great-Grandmother's shoulder. "I have many questions, Great-Grandmother."

"Ask me one tonight, Grandson, and the rest I'll answer in the morning," Great-Grandmother said sleepily.

"I have heard the story of the marriage many times, Great-Grandmother. When Mother and Grandmother tell the story, they tell it very differently. In their story, the skunk is jealous. She tries to prevent the marriage, but Little Thunder ends up marrying Shakes the Earth's daughter."

Great-Grandmother stroked Many Smiles' hair. "When I was little, I fell asleep by the stream. A skunk came and nestled with me. It was soft and gentle and had no fear. After that, I could not hear the story and imagine Skunk as an enemy. So I spoke to a Storyteller, and she told me that the First Stories are like bones without skin. Each person who tells a story can put a new skin on the story she tells.

"My story is still the story of Little Thunder's wedding. Little Thunder's feats at Shakes the Earth's village are still the same. Shakes the Earth still protects his daughter, and the creatures of the forest still help Little Thunder. But this way, Little Thunder marries a friend, and his friend does everything she can to protect him, even when it seems they will never be together. The skunk that snuggled up to me that night when I was a girl told me that this was the truth. The way the skunks tell it, Little Thunder and Open Path never gave up until they reached their hearts' desire. So I told the story this way."

Many Smiles felt his eyes grow heavy and he nestled close to Great-Grandmother's feet.

"My boy," she continued, "you carry the ancient stone, the Child of the Grandmother Rock. But you carry it in a bag that was made a short time ago. No one sees the stone when you wear it, all they see is the pouch. Someday, you may add quillwork and paint the pouch. But the stone inside will remain the same. I think stories are very much like that. At the heart, stone or bone, the first stories are still all there, unchanged. But each of us has the opportunity to create some wonderful pouch to hold the stone in. And that is precisely what I did when I told the old story in this way." Many Smiles carried those thoughts into his peaceful sleep.

2.6 *Land Tells a Story:*
Memory Techniques and Learning to Listen
to the Stories that the Land Tells

Many Smiles ran, dodging the many trees, the way a deer shifts direction in the forest. His hair flowed behind him and the wind was on his face. He felt Mother Earth under his bare feet. He knew that in this sacred forest was buried the last baby teeth of all his people, each at the base of a different tree. "You, rough-barked Oak, you who give Our People acorns! See my last baby tooth! Smooth-barked Beech, you that give Our People sweet nuts, look at this! My last baby tooth! Ash, whose root holds the baby tooth of my father! Look, this tooth is the child of the tooth that lies beneath your roots. Birch and Elm, which give Our People covering for our wigwams, Pines that feed us, a tooth, a tooth, a tooth!"

There stood Moose. His legs tensed and he prepared to bolt. He sensed that hunters were planning to search for his family.

He did not sense the pressure of the hunt in this young one. This child ran with a purpose, but what purpose? These hunters were odd creatures. They were covered mostly in light-brown frog skin. They covered their hooves in the skins of his herd, and they covered their legs in deer hide. They had manes—this one's black mane thrashed behind him as he ran. These were not proper moose manes, grown under the chin with dignity. No, these came out of the top of their heads. And then, on top of that mane, the moose observed that humans often wore moose hair, dyed red. In the winter, these creatures would even add a bear skin!

The moose had even asked a mosquito what she thought of these Two-Leggeds. She replied that their hides were thin and easy to bite, and while they may be put together with the parts of moose and deer and frog and bear and bird, they had no tails to shoo mosquitoes away. Clearly The Great Spirit created the Two-Leggeds especially to feed the mosquitoes.

Now here came this child. He was small and fast for a Two-Legged. He had no moose hide on his feet and no dyed mane in his hair. All he wore was two flaps of deerskin around his middle. He was waving something small. It looked like a pebble. He spoke to every tree as he ran, and the trees bowed their greetings to him, but none of them told the Two-Legged about the moose that was hiding in the forest watching him run from tree to tree.

Trees are not big talkers, and even the squirrels know that trees keep secrets better than any creature alive. That's why squirrels and chipmunks hide their acorns and beech nuts around trees. The moose stayed among the silent trees and observed the Two-Legged.

The thin, frog-skinned boy fell to his knees in front of a strong and most delicious young tree of the forest, the Black Birch. This particular Black Birch seemed to know the boy. Its topmost branch nodded ever so slightly toward him. The Two-Legged's strange front paws started clawing at the ground as if this creature had suddenly transformed into a raccoon or a nut-burying squirrel. At least this one was careful not to disturb the roots of the tree. Meanwhile, Blue Jay, who could not keep a secret, hopped to a branch on that same tree and shouted "Cat! Cat!" Blue Jay believed that all creatures that hunted were really bobcats in disguise, and if you asked him, he could explain why for hours. The mosquitoes heard Blue Jay, and gathered to feast.

Many Smiles left to hunt moose with the men the next morning.

"Be patient. Your feelings will guide you." This was the advice of Becomes Unseen. Up a hill, the hunting party walked. Becomes Unseen touched Many Smiles' shoulder with his fingertips to signal him to wait.

"I have a lesson to share with you, Nephew. It is the story the land tells. The part the Storyteller plays in the hunt is to remember how to tell the story of the way back to the village."

"And how do we do that?"

Becomes Unseen was not a Master Storyteller like Little Hawk, but he had something to teach.

"Well, I will show you, Nephew. It is part song, part story."

Becomes Unseen began to sing softly, allowing his silent footsteps to keep to the rhythm of his words:

> *Teach me, oh land! So that I may understand!*
> *Teach me how to listen to the things you have to say.*

"We stop here, Nephew, and let the others go ahead so that I may speak to you as they continue to move quietly. My uncle taught me this way of seeing that helped me lead my people home. And he taught me to walk very slowly in the hunt, and see with my deep senses. You know how to make rope by twisting two strands together, and by adding more rope material and twisting, you can make a rope as long as you like. We will make a Story Rope the same way. We will look high into the forest and look at what the shapes of the trees, rocks, and branches tell us."

"Uncle, why should we look high?" Many Smiles asked.

"Because high silhouettes can be seen against the night sky. Now, look over there. What picture does that fir tree draw?"

Many Smiles used his feelings and looked deep inside. "It looks like a man with the head of a lobster!"

"That's very good. Now, let's keep walking until we can barely see the lobster."

Just before the tree passed from view around a bend in the hilly land, above them on a rocky ledge they saw a bush that had been crushed by a boulder. "Uncle, if I use my feelings, I can see that the boulder and the bush form a giant spider."

"Excellent, Many Smiles! Now, just the same way we make rope, we twist the new creature we see with what the last creature we saw *does*. For instance, what was the landmark before this giant spider?"

"It was the lobster, Uncle."

Becomes Unseen smiled at the boy. "And what does the lobster do?"

"He hides in the shallows and gives us food," Many Smiles answered.

"Now we twist what a lobster *does* with the spider. I can feel a giant spider hiding in shallow water and giving us food. Do you see it, nephew?"

"I think so. Let's keep walking and try another one."

My wise uncle knows many things, Many Smiles told himself. *As much as I want to be with the hunters up ahead, I know that Uncle's lesson will teach me a way to help my people. Still, I hope I don't miss the hunt!*

They waded through the brush and ducked under catbrier, following the trail that the moose had made and that the hunters had followed. Soon, they could barely see the boulder and saplings that looked like a spider. In a clearing, a tree lay on the earth. Its tall branches reached into the sky. They looked like arms crossed over a sleeping head. The roots also now pointed toward the sky. They looked like the moccasins of a sleeping man.

"Now, child," Becomes Unseen said, pointing at the fallen tree. "Twist the sleeping grandfather into what a spider does."

"I picture my sleeping grandfather. He is the size of a spider, and while his eyes are closed, he's spinning a web on tiny legs. I *really* can see it, my gray-haired grandfather, eyes closed, happily sleeping, scurrying along between two branches on eight legs, making a web."

The idea made Many Smiles laugh. The game was fun.

> *Sleeping grandfather spins a web*
> *Like the spider*
> *Who hides under rocks*
> *And ends up in our cooking bowl*
> *Like a lobster, who leads us home.*

As they continued to walk, just before the sleeping grandfather vanished from view, Many Smiles saw another fallen tree, a birch whose tip extended over the water.

"All right, Uncle. This birch looks like a canoe. Now I need to twist the thing I see with what the last character can do, right?"

Many Smiles paused. Then, a smile came to his face. "When my grandfather sleeps, he may snore. Boy, can he snore! When he sleeps, I dream about the ancestral drums of the whole nation drumming during a thunder storm! Do I picture a canoe *snoring*?"

"Now you understand!" Becomes Unseen patted Many Smiles on the head.

Many Smiles felt encouraged.

"So, if I were to sing it like a song, I'd sing:

> *The canoe is snoring loud*
> *Like sleeping grandfather, spinning webs*

Like the spider
Who hides under rocks
And ends up in our bowl
Like a lobster, who leads us home.

And the hunters continued on, coming to an area that looked as if giants had built a fire pit. "Look! That's an enormous fire pit!" Many Smiles laughed. "You will ask me 'What does the canoe do?' Well, it floats and carries me along the river. So I imagine a fire pit floating and carrying me along."

The fire pit floats us along
Like the canoe that's snoring loud…

Many Smiles repeated every verse until he got to the lobster. Now Uncle and Nephew were walking faster. This memory game was easy and fun. Many Smiles saw three trees that grew so close together that they shared a single base. "These are three sisters. I twist three sisters into my storytelling rope. I ask what a fire pit does. Fire eats wood and gives off heat and glows with light. So, I'll imagine three sisters eating wood and glowing."

Sisters eat wood and glow at night
Like the fire pit floating us along
Like the canoe that's snoring loud…

"Uncle, I really like this game. I can remember every part of the path! What's next? I know sisters whisper to each other and make moccasins, and pound acorns into flour, and make wigwams. And I imagine that one day, I will marry such a sister."

At the top of a hill, the moose tracks led to a rock that was half-round like the silent Moon that lit the night sky. Many Smiles twisted the image of the Moon with the three sisters. "Three Moons floating in the sky, pounding acorns into flour. I have to choose one of the Moons for a wife. Who would it be? The Full, the Half, or the Invisible Moon? Is that right, Uncle, am I twisting the Moon with what the three sisters do?"

"You learn quickly, Many Smiles. You are eager to know and to master what I offer you. This makes me feel very happy."

"Wise Uncle of mine, do you think that some of the rope of stories are put there by the forest to remind us of *other* stories? I mean the fire pit that is a canoe is very much like Glooscap's canoe, and marrying the Moon is as unusual as marrying a skunk. Is the forest telling us the same stories in signs that we tell in words?"

"Well, since all stories come from the Grandmother Rock, I believe the forest must have heard the same stories we tell, but they tell them in their own way. I am just teaching you how to understand what the forest is already saying. Now can you sing each of the landmarks that will lead you home?"

> *Moon of three I choose to wed,*
> *Like sisters eating wood at night...*

Many Smiles sang the story rope all the way back to the lobster.

"Look over there!" Many Smiles shouted. "Even when we pass it! From all sides, do you see that stone that juts out into the river? Look, Uncle! It—it—it looks just like a turtle! Let's see, what does the Moon do? It *glows*!"

Becomes Unseen lifted his hand. "I would not use the word glow. It is too similar to what the fire does. You already have the sisters glowing. The strands will not twist together strongly when they are too similar to other strands. What else does the Moon do?"

"Well, the Moon becomes small and then grows large and full and changes the walk of the Great Water."

"Good," Becomes Unseen nodded.

> *Turtle that wanes and waxes*
> *And pulls the tide*
> *Like Moon of three I choose to wed*
> *Like sisters...*
> *...Like a lobster, who leads us home.*

"Nephew, you can twist a hundred of these strands together as long as you don't use the same action or character twice. You can have as many images as you choose, hundreds even, and you'll remember each one in reverse, so you can follow the trail as you return from the hunt. Now, we must move quietly, because we are getting very close."

Many Smiles had loved, loved, *loved* the game so much he had forgotten that they were on a moose hunt! Now they caught up to the other hunters.

Nearby stood three trees that looked like spears. One was broken. Many Smiles thought, *What does a turtle do? She pulls in her head and legs. These trees make me think of three spears that could pull themselves back into my fist, the way a turtle pulls in her head, but one of the spears is broken.* Many Smiles whispered to himself,

> *Spear that pulls into my fist*
> *Like a turtle that wanes*
> *And pulls the tide*
> *Like Moon of three…*
> *…Like a lobster, who leads us home.*

Together, the hunters crept along the water's edge to a swamp. At the mouth of the swamp, Many Smiles could see a cave. Near the cave, in the watery shallows, was the moose.

> *Cave flies and cuts and takes the moose*
> *Like a spear that pulls into my fist*
> *Like a turtle that wanes*
> *And pulls the tide*
> *Like Moon of three I choose to wed*
> *Like sisters eating wood at night*
> *Like the fire pit floating us along*
> *Like the canoe that's snoring loud*
> *Like sleeping grandfather, spinning webs*
> *Like the spider*
> *Who hides under rocks*
> *And ends up in our bowl*
> *Like a lobster, who leads us home.*
> *Teach me, my clan! So that I may understand!*
> *Teach me how to listen to the things you have to say.*
> *Teach me, Great Moose! So that I may understand!*
> *Teach me how to listen to what your path has taught.*

Sharing the hunt was good. The village would have food and clothing and tools, and all the hunters thanked the moose for these gifts. Many Smiles had a lesson, and his wise uncle was about to give him another, "Let your story lead us back home. Then, take some of the children, and some of the young men and women for protection in case the wolves decide to share this moose. Collect what's left, and bring it to the village."

"But Uncle, the story tells how to get home, but how can I remember the way from the village to the moose?"

"Do you remember the first character in our story?"

"Yes. It was the lobster-man."

"And what do lobsters do?"

"They hide under rocks and feed us."

"Just like…?"

"The spider!"

"And what does the spider do?"

Many Smiles opened his dark eyes wide in amazement. "I can—I can remember the path forward and backward!"

"Yes, Nephew. If the story rope is twisted strongly, you can use it from either end."

"And, and not only do we have meat and leather and bone that my people can make into useful things, I have characters that I can make into a story that I gathered myself from listening to the land."

> *Teach me, oh land! So that I may understand!*
> *Teach me how to listen to the things you have to say.*
> *Teach me, oh land! So that my people understand*
> *To teach the things you've taught me so we'll live in a good way.*

Many Smiles practiced reading landmarks and twisting them into stories to help him remember paths through the forest. But he was also a Storyteller, and he realized that just as his people collect herbs and roots and fruits to bring back to cook into a meal, he had collected characters from the land that he could cook into a story.

2.7 The Story that the Land told Many Smiles (based on The Moose Trail): Cooking the Story you Gather into a Meal

Clever Old Grandfather Moose had lived for many seasons of ice and snow and he had lived for many seasons of sun and heat. He loved living in the forest and was not ready to be hunted.

In the same forest lived a boy named Yellow Wing, who had lived for a few seasons of ice and snow and a few seasons of sun and heat. He had lost all his first teeth and felt that it was time to hunt moose.

Clever Old Grandfather Moose hid in the forest and observed Yellow Wing. "I think I will have some fun with this one," he said. As Yellow Wing buried his baby tooth at the foot of an elm tree, Clever Old Grandfather Moose walked up behind him and stamped the ground.

"I see you have become a man, Two-Legged. I know it is the way of your people that in order to become a husband, and to sit at the council of your people, you must first hunt one of my tribe."

Yellow Wing had been so busy imagining his first moose hunt and burying his last baby tooth, that Grandfather Moose had startled him. Yellow Wing jumped to his feet. "Grandfather Moose, wait here for me so I may get my spears and hunt you."

"I would wait, Two-Legged, but I dare not. The largest bull moose in all the world is chasing me. He is a menace to all moose because his mind races wildly like the storm wind tumbles the trees."

"Did you say *the largest bull moose in all the world*? And did you mean that I would help your herd if I were to hunt this moose?" Yellow Wing imagined how good he would feel if he were to bring home the greatest moose of all. His people had always told him that it was best to hunt with others, that the lessons of the hunt belong to all, including the animal that is hunted. But Yellow Wing wanted the lessons only for himself. He imagined his clan moving their village to share the bounty of this moose, and he imagined how thankful his people would be.

"I will protect you, Grandfather Moose. Show me where I can find the largest bull moose in all the world and I will hunt him."

Grandfather Moose laughed to himself. "Surely I have found the silliest Two-Legged in the forest! I know I can throw him off my trail." He leaned so close to Yellow Wing that Grandfather Moose's mane tickled Yellow Wing's ear. He whispered, as if what he had to say was a very important secret. "The last person to see the bull moose was a Two-Legged, like you. He is a man with the head of a lobster. Find him and you will find the moose."

Now in those days, Our People had not yet learned how to fish, so Yellow Wing was not quite sure what a lobster was and did not want to admit that he didn't know. He thanked Grandfather Moose and returned to his village, gathered up his spears—in those days Our People had no bows or arrows. His people greeted him warmly and invited him to hunt with them.

"I'm going to hunt alone," he said and went to find the man with the head of a lobster.

Yellow Wing searched for seven days. He survived on pemmican, water, and berries. He felt hungry and he had no luck. On the seventh night, right before sunrise, he decided to go home. Just at dawn, he felt the earth shake. He knew what an earthquake was, but perhaps it was his hunger, or just his desire to find the bull moose, or perhaps he was still half-dreaming, but he imagined that what he'd felt had been the footfalls of the biggest moose on Earth! He stood and began to run in the direction of the Great Water.

Now, just near the Great Water lived a clan of fishermen. They were very busy when Yellow Wing approached because one of their young men had been stung many, many times on the face by wasps. They were gathering red clay to soothe the swollen skin.

When the Clan Mother saw Yellow Wing, so tired and hungry, she welcomed him into the wigwam. She gave him a delicious, salty stew he'd never tasted. Soon Yellow Wing was sleeping. When he awoke the Sun still shone high in the sky, and all the people were gone from the wigwam. All but one: lying on a skin near him was a...a creature. He had a young man's body, but his head was large, and covered with a reddish-colored shell! Of course, this was the boy who had clay on his swollen face to soothe the wasp stings, whose name was Little Crow. Perhaps it was that Yellow Wing was still half-dreaming, or perhaps it was just his desire to find the bull moose, but he was convinced he'd found the lobster-headed man!

"I seek what Grandfather Moose told me you would know how to find. I have traveled far to find you, so that you may tell me your secret, so that I may hunt it and bring its meat back to my tribe."

Little Crow imagined that the stranger was talking about a *person* named Grandfather Moose, who was probably a powerful Puoin and so knew the secrets of Little Crow's heart. The Puoin must know that Little Crow and his father had a special spot where they went to fish together, and there they could gather the biggest, and the most delicious crabs. Little Crow never imagined that this boy intended to hunt moose; nobody hunted moose alone.

"A half-day's walk down the sandy beaches to the south, what you seek for your people you will find. But this spot is special to my father and me. Please bring what meat you can carry to your people, but I ask you to promise me not to return to that spot again."

Yellow Wing agreed, and he thanked the young man with the lobster head, and he gathered his spears, and he thanked the clan mother for her hospitality, and insisted that it was time for him to go. She gave him two skins of fresh water and welcomed him to visit anytime. Yellow Wing's footprints pressed the sands heading south. He walked quickly, and at times he almost ran. He continued walking until in the distance he saw a large rock far from the shore. He remembered that the lobster-headed man had told him that he should wait for the rock to emerge from the water. Maybe that's when the bull moose came to that rock. He closed his eyes and went to sleep. The sounds of the ocean were soothing, and the Sun's early rays danced on his eyelids before he woke again.

Now the rock stood in the sand. Yellow Wing did not see an enormous moose. Perhaps he should hide by the rock and wait for the moose to come. Yellow Wing hid in a bit of shallow water just beyond the rock. As he moved his spear and shifted his feet, something bit him. He did a startled dance, and saw the creature that had bitten him. Yellow Wing had never seen a crab before, so to him this was a spider, a water spider, and the biggest spider he had ever seen.

"Great Water Spider, I mean you no harm. I am here to hunt the biggest bull moose on Earth. The lobster-headed man told me I could find him here."

The crab was confused. "I am no spider. I throw no web. I have lived through many scorching hot summers and freezing cold winters, and I have never seen a moose at my rock. But I have seen a creature, a Two-Legged like yourself who throws a web like a spider. I call him Grandfather Spider. He floats upon the water, throws his web, and sleeps. He has lived through more scorching hot summers and freezing cold winters than I have. If anyone knows where to find your moose, surely it is Grandfather Spider. Now I can see you are a hunter. If you take the time to learn from me and my tribe, we could teach you what we know about the food of the sea, and you would not have to worry about chasing a giant moose."

"Thank you Sea Spider, and I hope you enjoy the bite you took out of my toe. But I hunt moose and I will not rest until I find what I seek."

Yellow Wing walked down the beach. His head was down and his heart was heavy. The sky was large, and the wind threw sand in his face. The Sun dried his skin. He took a gulp of water, given to him by the kind clan mother. For the first time in his life, he felt lonely. This thirst for other people was almost as powerful as his thirst for water. His quest for the great bull moose now seemed silly. Maybe his people were wise to hunt together. Still, he wanted the lessons of the hunt only for himself, and he had come so far, he had to see his journey through.

He came upon a tiny wigwam, not even big enough for one family. Sitting near the wigwam, he saw an elder. When the man looked up and saw Yellow Wing, he did not greet him with the customary kindness. Instead, he rudely snapped, "What do you want?"

"I am a moose hunter. I seek the biggest bull moose in the world."

"Where is your hunting party?"

"I hunt alone."

The years and the Sun and the salt and a great sadness had aged this grandfather.

"Sit with me, Young Moose Hunter. Help me mend my nets, and let me teach you something. I am from The Land of the Snoring Canoe, so-called because our waters are so full of fish that we throw our nets and sleep, and when we wake, the fish have filled our nets. I was once as young as you are now, but that was many, many, *many* blazing hot summers and freezing cold winters gone by. I decided that I would fish alone, so that the lessons of the catch would be mine alone. I bragged that I would bring in so many fish by myself that my canoe would sink. I still have not made that catch and I feel ashamed to return to my people. You are the first visitor I have had since my hair turned gray, many seasons ago."

The lonely man taught Yellow Wing how to tie a net. More importantly, he taught Yellow Wing that it might be a foolish thing to hunt alone and not to want to share his lessons with others. Yellow Wing spent a day on the sea with the lonely man and, when the man threw his net, Yellow Wing understood how the crab could confuse this tall thin man and his net with a spider.

The fishing was easy. The catch was abundant. That night by the fire, Yellow Wing told the lonely man about the crab. He was careful not to reveal the secret location because he had promised the lobster-headed young man to keep it a secret.

"Crabs are patient creatures. You should have accepted that crab's offer. They can teach you many things."

"After I return to my people with the great bull moose, I will lead a hunting party to this shore and you can teach my people how to fish, and you will be our grandfather."

The fish hunter sighed. "So you will continue to hunt your moose despite my experience. Well, I wish I could help you. All I know is that a day's walk from here, maybe more, you will reach the Land of the Snoring Canoe. Maybe my people have seen the bull moose. I wish you the best, but I ask you to consider in everything you do, is what you are giving up worth what you might get?"

Yellow Wing promised to consider all the fish hunter had told him. He was anxious to find out what the Elder's people knew of the bull moose. He also planned to tell them of that gray-haired, lonely man in his small wigwam. A day later, when he finally arrived and explained where he'd been, the elders rejoiced and sent runners to bring the fish hunter home.

They invited Yellow Wing to stay and to join in the welcome home celebration. Yellow Wing agreed to stay. The Chief told Yellow Wing that he was as likely to find a fire pit floating on the ocean as to find such a big bull moose. Yellow Wing joined the tribe and helped fish for the feast. Sure enough, The People threw their nets in the water, lay down in their canoes and waited, until many canoes floated on the water, snoring. When the Sun cast the shortest shadow the next day, the runners arrived with their long-lost fish hunter. The village celebrated more than they had ever celebrated before.

"See?" the Puoin told the no-longer-lonely man, "You do not need to bring home fish to celebrate. Because we knew you were returning to us, we caught more fish than we've ever caught before! Our catch could sink a canoe!" The fish hunter was no longer lonely. He thanked Yellow Wing.

"I am happy to help. Now I leave to find the floating fire pit that your Chief spoke of. There, I will find word of the bull moose."

In his heart, Yellow Wing knew he no longer wished to hunt alone. The Sun set on the water, just beyond a tiny island. The orange glow of the setting Sun reflected off the wet rocks on the tiny island, until that island looked just like a fire pit on the ocean. *It was the floating fire pit!* Yellow Wing thought he should make one last try to find the bull moose. He jumped into the ocean and swam, but the currents were strong. He thrashed and swallowed water and went under. When he reached the cold, rocky island, night had already painted the sky. Yellow Wing could see no bull moose on the island and besides, he'd lost his spears in the struggle against the current. Disheartened, cold, and lonely, he fell asleep.

Just before sunrise, Yellow Wing saw the three sister stars that shone over his home, shining also here, far away. "I will marry one of your earthly sisters," he told the stars, "someone who will show me the way home, and remind me never to wander so far in search of such foolish things." Even though it was dark, the Moon swam brightly on the surface of the water like a turtle. In fact, the Moon took the form of a turtle and spoke to Yellow Wing. "Do you realize that fishing, the gift that you bring to your people, is greater than the gift of the largest moose? Do you realize that what you have learned from your journey will help feed your people, and their children and grandchildren beyond the Seventh Generation?"

The tide had receded from the shore, and Yellow Wing could follow the moonlight through the wet sand to the forest. He dried himself in the rays of the rising Sun.

In the wet sand, he found his three spears washed up among the grasses and rocks. One spear had somehow been broken. This was a sign. He was returning home from the hunt with his hands empty, but his mind and his heart were full.

He followed the trails homeward. He walked for two days. Then, on the morning of the third day, he heard a commotion and followed it to the mouth of a cave, where the trembling of the earth had loosed many rocks and had trapped something inside. He dug through the rubble, and to his amazement, after he had cleared the cave, there stood—thin and thirsty, dusty and weak—the same moose that had set him on his journey in the first place.

Clever Old Grandfather Moose looked at Yellow Wing and heaved a heavy sigh of moose gratitude. "I deceived you, young hunter, in order to live. I lied to you. There is no enormous bull moose."

Yellow Wing laughed. "You are right. There is no bull moose. But there is a lobster-headed man, and a water spider, and a grandfather spider and a snoring canoe, and a fire pit that floats on the water, and three sisters in the sky, and a moon-turtle and an empty hand, and a broken spear, and a cave that throws itself like a spear. But most of all, there is a journey, and there are my people, and there are new lessons I take to them, thanks to you, Grandfather Moose."

Three

LIFTING THE UNDERSTANDING:

Lessons of Coming of Age[2]

3.1 We Have Many Faces:
Self-Awareness and Other Awareness

When was the Sun going to rise? Many Smiles woke before his hosts, and lay awake waiting for the others to stir—he was so sure that the day would bring great things. He had hardly slept the night before. He twisted left and right on his sleeping mat. Now quietly, he crawled to the entrance of the wigwam of his hosts Gray Dog, the daughter of Dancing Rain, and her husband, Howling Wolf—the Puoins of the village.

Many Smiles crept under the door flap. He felt the deer hide brush his back. The light was weak in the sky, but the birds were already singing dawn songs. Through the darkness, he could see a shadow approach. It was Seagull, the daughter of the Puoin, carrying clean bowls from the river. She was the same girl he had known as Playful Otter the first time he visited the village. She wore her hair long and loose, like all the children. She smiled and crouched next to Many Smiles. Together, silently, they sat and watched dawn explode over the sky, the tribe awaken, and the animals greet the coming of the day.

When the Sun had risen, Seagull and Many Smiles walked to the wigwam of Little Hawk and Dancing Rain. When they arrived, they stood respectfully at the lowest post in the wigwam. In the manner of children not fully grown, they stood until they were invited to sit. Then they would have knelt upright so that their heads were at the same level as the adults, but Little Hawk and Grandmother Dancing Rain did not motion for Many Smiles to sit. Instead, the two Storytellers came to the doorway of the wigwam and hugged Seagull and Many Smiles. They embraced Many Smiles and called him *Grandson*.

Many Smiles had come to this place to learn and he realized he'd just learned his first lesson: *The great gift of these two Storytellers is that they say the everyday things the Ancestors have said for many hundreds of years, but when these two speak, all those words seem new as if invented by them and spoken for the first time.* Many Smiles greeted *Grandmother* Dancing Rain and *Grandfather* Little Hawk, and felt the words *Grandmother* and *Grandfather* with all of his heart.

"You are welcome to sit at the highest post, my children. You are welcome to sit wherever you choose in this wigwam and you should not feel uncomfortable. A Storyteller has to fill the whole space of the wigwam, so you as a Storyteller must move about freely."

Many Smiles and Seagull sat next to Little Hawk and Dancing Rain, and Dancing Rain offered them both a stew of venison and grape leaves. The lemony taste of the grape leaves perfectly complemented the meat.

"Now," Little Hawk spread his hands wide. "Tell me about your journey here."

"I live one day's walk..." Many Smiles began.

"Please forgive me. I interrupt as your teacher." Dancing Rain's voice was firm, but gentle. "I will tell you a secret about storytelling. When I told my first stories to my people, I was frightened, so I focused my attention on my own small children.

"Instantly, I could feel how my energy grew, how my body moved forward, how my voice changed when I spoke to those tiny children. Then, I noticed that everyone, old and young, was smiling.

"This is because within every human, old or young, a child lives. It is to this child that I speak when I tell a story. My voice tells the child within each person that it is good to come out and play. When I tell my stories, I can see the child awakening in the faces of old and young alike, and the room instantly fills with the energy, love, and magic of childhood. Do not speak to us, speak to the children in our hearts."

Many Smiles thanked Grandmother Dancing Rain for the teaching and began again, imagining his listeners as children, and loving them, laughing with them.

"Just like you, I live in a wigwam. Just like your people, my people hunt and fish. Like your people, we have a wise Clan Mother. We have grandfathers to teach us the ways of Our People. We have cousins, who wrestle us and hunt with us and play games with us. We have brothers and sisters and we have our father and our uncles and our mother."

Many Smiles paused and looked at his listeners. "Every boy knows that his mother is as loving as any mother in his village and that she has known him before he even knew himself. Every boy knows that he has a wise grandfather and that his father and uncle are great hunters, and that they have shared with him their wisdom and have fed him since before he can remember. Every member of every tribe knows that their Clan Mother has knowledge we can all call upon. When I left my village, I was going to a place where most people were unknown to me, where the mothers would only now meet me for the first time, where fathers and uncles would only now be sharing their wisdom with me. I was going to a place where someone else's grandfather would know the ways of some other people. I was going to a place where some other Clan Mother would have a knowledge that was far and wide.

"I left my wigwam to begin my journey, and tears came with me. I said goodbye to everyone…everyone except my uncle, Becomes Unseen. He was nowhere to be found. I guess he had become unseen."

This part is too long, Many Smiles thought, *and it's too sad. What can I say to break the mood?*

"The big, white, burning hot Sun in the sky soon dried my tears and the birds sang for me, and the chipmunks wrestled in the bush, and the shy deer kept careful eyes on me, and I was happy because I was going away to become a Storyteller. So I made myself small. I ran and jumped on all fours like a chipmunk, and I spread my arms and I flew like a bird, and the fawns looked at me, foolish human that I was, and then the young deer looked at each other and then they looked at me again. I ran towards them and leaped. They disappeared, running back to their deer mommies to tell of the strange creature they had seen dancing in the woods."

Well, better, but I need more energy.

"I was going to learn from two of the greatest Storytellers I had ever heard. And someday I would return to my village as a Storyteller. I was going to see my friend, Playful Otter, so I asked the birds to fly ahead and tell her that I was coming.

"In the sky, a seagull laughed. 'Whenever you go away from something you love, you feel sad. Whenever you go toward something you love, you feel happy,' the seagull told me.

"Many summers ago, when I last visited this village I came on short legs. The journey took me two days on such little legs. This time, I wanted to arrive as fast as the deer could arrive, as fast as the seagulls, or as the clouds floating fast on the winds. I wanted, wanted, *wanted* to get to the village of the great Storytellers. I wanted, wanted, *wanted* to begin my training. And I didn't want to think of the sadness of leaving my village.

"Every rock and tree reminded me of someone I knew. My imagination is always working, working hard with many thoughts that are like ants. They can pick up an idea—a big idea—and carry it, and then go back for another idea, and another, and another.

"My hardworking imagination told me that I was not alone. Each time the wind picked up, a bush would rustle close by. Each time I ran and stopped quickly, I imagined I heard footsteps behind me. I had the sense that someone or something was trailing me. You know the feeling when the small hairs on your arms stand to warn you because something is not right? That's what I felt. My eyes grew wide and my hearing grew sharp. The Sun was so bright that it turned everything bluish. Even when I closed my eyes, a blue spot remained. The air smelled sharp. There was a hunger in it.

"This was not my imagination. Something *was* following me.

"My knees felt soft, like they were asking to run. I am a quick runner and I do not tire easily. I ran. I knew I would reach a river, and the river would be difficult to cross silently. I ran faster. I imagined I could hear feet running behind me. I ran *even* faster. My heart sounded a quick drumbeat in my ears and my chest squeezed tight from breathing so hard. What came behind me? Was I being chased by some creature who hoped to make me its meal?

"I kept running, and the wind in my face made me feel good even as my imagination made me feel frightened. The strength of my body made me feel good even as the thought of being chased made me feel frightened. The warm Sun on my face made me feel good even as the eyes at my back made me feel frightened.

"And I reached the river. And I waited. And what did I see? No one. And what did I smell? Just the river, and even my own sweat. And in the river, what did I feel? I felt the coolness of the water. And I put my mouth to the water, and what did I taste? I tasted the cold, sweet river. And what did I hear?

"I heard a splash. Splash! And as quickly as I could, I scrambled up the bank. I began to run. What else did I hear? I heard my name. I knew the voice. And what did I do? What could I do? I stopped running. I sat in the sand. I laughed.

"Out of the water came my uncle, Becomes Unseen."

Many Smiles paused in the story. *They must remember this name!*

"Say the name with me, please…Out of the water came my uncle…"

Many Smiles used his arms to prompt his small group of listeners to say his uncle's name. He crossed his arms over his face to make himself *unseen*, and then peeked one eye out behind his crossed arms. He did it again. He crossed his arms in front of his face and said in a loud voice, "Becomes…" and then he peeked an eye out, and said in a tiny voice, "Unseen." He prompted Grandfather Little Hawk, Grandmother Dancing Rain, and Seagull to say it with him.

"Becomes Unseen is my wonderful uncle. I threw my arms around him, I was so happy to see him and I shouted with joy.

"My uncle smiled at me. 'You know, my Nephew, that my name, (say it with me) *Becomes Unseen*, means that you will not always see me when I'm there.'

"'Yes, my Uncle.'

"'You know something else? My full name is (say the first part with me) Becomes Unseen *and* We Have Many Faces.'"

(Here Many Smiles pointed to all the faces in wigwam.)

"'I didn't know that, my Uncle,' I said.

"'You know something more, my Nephew? Because you are so dear to me, I will often visit you, but you may not always know I'm there. I may appear as a child, or an elder, or as a girl, or as a deer, or as a dog, or a tree.'

"'But if you appear as a child, or as an elder, or as a girl, or as a deer, or as a dog, or a tree, how will I know that it is you? Because you are so dear to me, I'll always want to know.'

"'But you *may not* know. I suppose all you can do is to treat everyone as if they are your beloved relative and that you are overjoyed to see them.'

"My uncle (say it with me!) Becomes Unseen is a great hunter because he can make himself unseen. He says the secret to invisibility is to blend your body and spirit in such a way that you are one with all life. Being a part of life is more beautiful than being separate. He says that the better the still pond reflects the sky, the better it protects the fish deep below the surface.

"When I am with my uncle, I am the bright sky and the Sun and the well-drawn clouds. The way he reflects me makes me feel interesting and beautiful. He thinks that makes him unseen, but it really does just the opposite. I *always* see him, every time I feel interesting and wonderful. He is here, because the fire is beautiful and draws my attention. He is here because you, Grandfather Little Hawk and Grandmother Dancing Rain, greeted me as family. He is here because right now I feel like the beloved nephew of all creation.

"So, (say it with me) Becomes Unseen and We Have Many Faces and I walked together for awhile, and talked, mostly about moose tracks, and fishing, and of important things that uncles can explain to nephews. I can't tell you when he left me, or if he left me, or if he's still here now. All I know is that by the time I crossed the second river, he had vanished.

"I know about tracking and, maybe if I had gone back, I would have learned the secrets of his invisibility from his tracks in the leaves. But I am not a tracker or shape-shifter. I am a Storyteller, and my uncle (once more, all together) Becomes Unseen and We Have Many Faces had given me the gift of this story that I tell to you now, and I give to you the gift of imagining for yourself if he went back or if he is still here with me. I came into the village and was greeted happily by the Puoins, Gray Dog and Howling Wolf, who are Seagull's parents. I was also greeted by Seagull's brothers. They are, all of you are, after all, my beloved relatives and…We Have Many Faces."

3.2 The Best Fish:
Creating Plots That Respond to Other Plots — "Braiding" Plots Together

"Two weeks have passed since you have come to be with us, Grandson Many Smiles. We are happy to have you. You are learning quickly. I was thinking about this: Did you know that when I was a child, Dancing Rain and I lived in the same village as your grandfather, Deer Cloud? That was long, long ago. I am sure your grandfather has told you something about it."

"He mentioned that you were there—younger than he was—but that you and he became friends, and that your grandfather was a great fish hunter."

"My grandfather…," Little Hawk laughed. "My grandfather would have disagreed. But I believe he was the greatest fish hunter I ever met. Would you like to hear how he became great?"

"Oh yes, very much."

"This is the story of my Grandfather, Keeps Watch, and Our People, and The Great Decision. This story taught me a very important lesson about how to tell a story, you know."

Little Hawk moved his hand over the fire and blew. Immediately, a great fireball burst out of the fire pit and then, in a flash, it was gone!

"This was the summer after the Great Fire," Little Hawk said. "The black-trunked trees were being reborn with tiny branches and leaves, and the ferns felt extra sunlight on the forest floor. Our People left the winter village early because the moose and deer had not recovered. The elders decided to go to the Great Water early that year to fish. This was in a time where Grandfather Keeps Watch was about your age, and not yet a man. You can guess what he thought about most of the time…"

"Becoming a man!" Many Smiles declared.

"You know this because that is what you think about a lot, isn't it?" Little Hawk laughed and gently poked Many Smiles.

"Yes, Grandfather Little Hawk."

"And why do you think about becoming a man?"

"So I can do the things that men do, like, like, sit at council, and help with decisions, sit high in the wigwam and, well…"

"And so you can think about getting married?"

Many Smiles nodded. "*Think about*, Grandfather, not *do*. I still have many seasons as an unmarried man."

"Well, Grandfather Keeps Watch was very much in love with Snow Moved by Wind, and she was a Puoin, and a hunter, and as beautiful as her name. Her voice was the music of the birds to Keeps Watch, and her hair was the shiny black of a bear coming out of the sparkling river to Keeps Watch, and her smile was the glow of a fire as it is breathed into flame to Keeps Watch. And often, very often that glow would secretly shine at him, and he would smile at her. And his smile was the warm sand on a summer day to my grandmother.

"Keeps Watch was supposed to become a man that spring, in the final moose hunt. The Great Fire had made the moose scarce. No moose could be hunted until the herd recovered. Keeps Watch would have to wait to take his first moose, and he'd have to wait to become a man. He could not sit at the council, he could not help with the decisions, he could not sit high in the wigwam, and…"

Little Hawk looked at Many Smiles and prompted him to answer.

"…He could not marry your grandmother."

"This was a problem. But Keeps Watch understood that the council was wise and the herd was more important than his desires. Before the village moved to the fishing grounds, the elders gathered to discuss an important new idea. Most of those on the council thought the new idea was good and they decided to discuss it again, so that those who did not think it was a good idea could have time to consider their opinions and voice their concerns. What was this idea? Keeps Watch felt curious, but he knew that the council would tell him and the other children at the proper time.

"That summer, Keeps Watch threw his net, and the spirit of the Great Water told him to pull the net back quickly. The quick motion snagged the gill and one fin of the largest, most delicious-looking fish Keeps Watch had ever seen. In fact, it was as big as a moose! But it was very heavy, and it wasn't secure in the net. Keeps Watch struggled; he called for the whole village to help him. He even threw his body over the fish and hugged it, wrestled it into the canoe. The fish slithered, and flipped and slapped its tail and flopped back to the water.

That summer Keeps Watch worked hard. He spent many hours pulling his nets and throwing his spears. He caught many fish, and learned from his elders to be strong and silent and swift. Our People dried the catch and ate well, thanks to Keeps Watch. And in the cold of winter, after the fish had all been eaten, in the time of hunger before the bears awaken, he closed his eyes and imagined his mother cooking that big fish that had gotten away; he dreamed about the fish, he could even taste its sweet meat in his dreams!

"The council met at the Full Moon, when the sap had started to flow in the birch and maple trees."

"'This has been a difficult winter. We must thank the Water Nation for our survival,' the Chief said.

"'As difficult as it was for us, it was more difficult for the wolves. They had a hard time finding weak moose. Many nights I could hear them call to the Great Spirit for food. It was also a difficult time for the moose. The forest will need more time to recover, and we need to leave moose hunting for our neighbors, the wolves. They are great hunters, but we are better at catching fish, and we can dry our meat. We must wait another season for our brothers the moose to recover before we can help them thin the herds again,' said an elder.

"The council had not allowed a moose hunt for two winters. The hungry cries of the neighbors, the wolves, were less than they had been, but the flow had not yet been restored. Another year would go by without the moose hunt.

"You can imagine how Keeps Watch felt. All that winter, he tracked the moose, practiced moving silently, and threw spears at targets. He studied the wolves and organized his own circle of boys who had also been waiting to take their first moose. Together, they learned to move silently and swiftly and undetectably through the recovering brush. Keeps Watch decided that if he could not bring a moose home for his people, at least he could bring stories of the moose.

"In a similar manner, they learned to stalk the wolf neighbors, and learned their hunting techniques. They came to understand the wolves' language so that now the howls and barks told these young men where the moose were. From all of their activity, these young men realized that the flow in the balance was not yet complete. And that spring, it was they who told their elders that the moose hunt would have to wait another year. The young men could not sit at council, could not help with the decisions, could not sit high in the wigwam, and..."

"Could not marry."

"That was a problem. It was not an easy decision for Grandfather Keeps Watch, counseling the elders to wait. You see, Keeps Watch was very much in love with Snow Moved by Wind, and she was a wonderful Puoin and hunter, and was as beautiful as her name. And her voice was the gentle beating of a warm summer rain on the wigwam roof. And her hair was as black as the sky over the Great Water on the night of the Empty Moon. And her smile was the dawn over the Great Water. And to Keeps Watch, very often that dawn would secretly rise just for him. And like the Great Water itself, his smile would be the reflection of the Eastern Sun on the waves.

"Just before Our People moved to the summer village, the men gathered at council to discuss the new idea. They had made adjustments, taking into account the wisdom of those who had disagreed. Now the women needed to speak and add their wisdom to the council. They agreed to speak of the idea again in the next season.

"Now you understand the pattern of the days. Each year was the same. Our young hunters grew stronger, Keeps Watch's love for Snow Moved by Wind grew stronger, Keeps Watch fed Our People while searching for the Great Fish, and in the winter, he feasted many times on the imagined meal. Seven years had passed since the Great Fire. That fall, the young hunters listened to the wolves, and they agreed that it was time.

"By now Keeps Watch's circle of hunters was so good at stalking moose that they could have easily become men in a single moon. But this was not best for the moose. In seven years, many young men had come to the time of adulthood, they had all joined Keeps Watch's circle. Together they decided Keeps Watch should lead the hunt. His time of waiting was over.

"Soon afterward, one dark winter night, as Keeps Watch, the newlywed, sat high in his own wigwam facing his beloved wife, he told her of the great fish and the feast. He had imagined that meal so many times, that when he told the story, Snow Moved by Wind could taste the fish, and she fell asleep with her belly as full as if she had feasted all day.

"That spring, the District Chief visited the Council and the Clan Mother. The District Chief promised to consider the new idea, and said that he would return the next year. A year passed. Children were born. Keeps Watch became a father for the first time. Grandfather had almost everything a person could want, yet the great fish still eluded him. Loved ones went to the Fires of the Ancestors and, in the coldest days of winter, Snow Moved by Wind asked her husband to tell her the story of the feast of the great fish. The years passed, councils met, children were born, and more loved ones went to the Fires of the Ancestors. The Grand Chief of all the districts approved the decision of the Grand Council. What was this decision? Be patient, and I will tell you.

"Each year, Grandfather Keeps Watch would tell his growing family the story of the feast. Each year, he would hunt for the great fish and he taught his children to do the same. Each year, the fish eluded them all.

"When Keeps Watch became a grandfather—when I was born—the council finally announced the decision. Our village had grown, and it was time to form a new village and to set aside hunting grounds and fishing areas for that new village. Grandfather Keeps Watch's circle of young men were now elders but no one had forgotten Grandfather's leadership. It was decided that he should be chief of the new village.

"We came here, one day's walk from your village. Grandfather was a great Chief and my grandmother a great Puoin. Dancing Rain was born two years after I was. I learned much about storytelling from the story of the feast Grandfather Keeps Watch told. And every year, when we moved to our summer village, he hoped that this would be the year he caught that fish.

"Another year passed. People hunted, children were born, and just before I was ready to become a man, the ancestors called Grandmother Snow Moved by Wind to tend their fires. I loved Grandfather Keeps Watch very much and I noticed that often, after she was gone, he would leave the village."

"'Where have you gone, Grandfather?'

"'I have gone to hear your grandmother's voice.'

"'But Grandfather, how can you hear Grandmother's voice?'

"'Long ago, when we waited for my time to become a man, her voice was like the song of birds and the gentle beating of the summer rain on the roof of the wigwam. I waited nine years to marry her, but for forty-nine years of my life I have heard her voice in these beautiful things. Now, when I hear the song of birds and the gentle beating of the summer rain on the roof of the wigwam, she speaks to me.'

"Another time, I would ask, 'Where have you gone, Grandfather?'

"'I have gone to admire your grandmother's beautiful hair.'

"'But Grandfather, how can you admire Grandmother's beautiful hair?'

"'Long ago, when I waited for my time to become a man, your grandmother's hair was as shiny black as a bear coming out of the sparkling river, as black as the night sky over the Great Water on the night of the Empty Moon. I waited nine years to marry her, but for forty-nine years of my life

I have seen her hair in these beautiful things. Now, when I see a bear coming out of the sparkling river, or see the night sky over the Great Water on the night of the Empty Moon, I see her hair.'

"Another time, I would ask, 'Where have you gone Grandfather?'

"'I have gone to smile with your grandmother."

"'But Grandfather, how can you smile with Grandmother?'

"'Long ago, when we waited for my time to become a man, her smile was the glow of a fire as it is breathed into flame. It was the dawn over the Great Water. Now, when I feel a spark of fire as it is breathed into flame, or feel the dawn over the Great Water, I feel her smile.'

"And then, Grandfather smiled back at me.

"'But mostly, Little Hawk, I see her in your father and your aunts and uncles and your cousins and you and your sister, Dancing Rain.' Then he smiled at me and said, 'Every time I feel the warm sand on a summer day, or the reflection of the Eastern Sun on the water, I will know the feeling of her smile.'

"He never stopped trying to catch the great fish, and sixty years after it had escaped, one summer day, he felt a tug at his net. We heard the splashing, we watched Grandfather wrestle, and our whole family, our whole *village* paddled out to help. The great fish had grown almost to the size of a small whale, but it was ancient and no longer very strong. Between all of us, we were ready to catch that fish and finally have the feast. And Grandfather raised a hand, and then took out his knife. To our horror, he cut away the net, and we watched the fish swim away to sea.

"'But Grandfather!' we all protested.

"'Swim, my Brother. Now I have had the chance to do what I set out to do, to thank you. You were the teacher who taught me never to give up. You taught me patience and hard work. You fed my imagination for sixty years and provided me with great feasts even in times of hunger. You have fed my wife, my children, and my grandchildren. Your spirit moves in me, and mine moves in you.' Then he turned to us. 'Let's bring the boats back to shore. It's time for a feast.'"

Dancing Rain listened to Little Hawk's story while she braided Seagull's hair. "Do you understand why this story is like this braided hair? Three separate stories braided together teach a single important lesson about storytelling."

"And what lesson is that?" Many Smiles asked.

Dancing Rain laughed. "If we tell you that, you will have eaten the fish."

Many Smiles felt frustrated by this answer. "But Grandmother!" he protested.

"Think about it, Grandson. What is the storytelling lesson?"

For weeks afterwards, Many Smiles puzzled over the story, discussed it with Seagull, and presented his ideas to Grandfather and Grandmother.

"Let nothing discourage you!" he suggested.

"This is a good lesson, Grandson, but it isn't *the* lesson."

Another week went by. "Is it about patience and hard work?"

"Another good lesson, but not *the* lesson."

Time passed. Occasionally, Seagull and Many Smiles would discuss the story, and try to figure out *the* storytelling lesson. Did the grandchildren figure out the meaning to the story? Keep reading. I promise I will tell you if they did.

3.3 Three Stories:
How the Caretaker Cues the Storyteller

(Dancing Rain prompts Little Hawk to tell
three stories to Many Smiles and Seagull.)

Many Smiles and Seagull relaxed with heavy eyelids after a delicious meal. Dancing Rain sat by the fire. She handed Little Hawk a conch shell.

Grandfather blew on the conch shell and the two young Storytellers jumped. The sound was so loud, it seemed to even startle the fire.

Little Hawk began to tell a story. "My children, I want you to repeat after me, *Our People do not waste.*

"When I was very little, my grandmother taught me how to get food from these shells. The food was very delicious, and I was very happy to have it."

Little Hawk turned the conch shell over in his hands. "This shell is much larger than the ones I found as a child. Our People traveled far South along the coast by canoe to find this shell. I remember making this journey in a long canoe with twenty-eight others. The Great Water was rough, and it tossed our canoe towards land, and we came to a place that had no birchbark. But we found people there who acted like our brothers and showed us the bark of a tall, straight tree that we used to repair our canoe." Little Hawk paused.

"When I was very young, I was helping my grandmother to take the sweet meat from the shells. I watched her fill a basket with the empty shells."

"'Little one, please carry this basket and empty it on the mound of shells,' my grandmother asked me.

"Once again, my children, I want you to repeat after me, *Our People do not waste.*

"The young ones sometimes have difficulty understanding the ways of The People. In my mind, these shells were nothing special, just something that once contained delicious food. So I decided not to walk all the way to the shell pile and instead, I emptied the basket nearby. I returned quickly to my grandmother, who looked at me in a way that told me I had done something wrong."

Grandfather looked sternly at Many Smiles and Seagull. He said nothing, just waited for the emotion to build, like a seed taking root. In the silence, the listeners felt that same guilty feeling that Little Hawk must have felt as a child. The feeling was so genuine that they both laughed.

"I remind you, my children," Little Hawk said, "*Our People do not waste.* Please say it with me, *Our People do not waste.*

"My grandmother asked me, 'Little Hawk, my Grandson, you have returned so quickly from the shell pile. Did you run all the way there?'

"I lowered my eyes. 'Grandmother, what difference does it make where I place the shells? I just put them out back near the wigwam.'

"Grandmother looked at me.

"'Grandson Little Hawk, you must know that the wisdom of your people is an ancient wisdom. I want you to go back to the place where you threw away the shells and collect them, and then place them on the great pile of shells, where Our People and the neighboring clans have been placing their shells since the time of the Great-Grandfathers of the Ancestors.'"

Grandfather Little Hawk studied the shell in his hands. "I look at this shell and it reminds me of the wisdom I learned from my grandmother that day. I went back to the pile of shells I had carelessly discarded. The odor was strong!

"The meat that was left over in the shell had become food for a cloud of flies that decided that my arms might also be tasty. I threw some sand over the shells to scatter the flies, and I asked the flies not to bite me. Maybe I did not speak their language very well, because by the time I collected all the shells I had dumped, my back was filled with welts where the flies had bitten me. Grandmother brought a covered basket and we put the shells in this basket. Together we walked to the large pile of shells. It was a long walk.

"'Grandson,' she said, 'your small legs are very fast. Now we have arrived at the great pile of shells. Look around you, what do you see?'"

Little Hawk's voice softened. "I saw our own people, and people from other clans digging in the pile of shells. Some were respectfully removing tools of bone and antler that had been buried in the pile.

"'These bones and antlers were buried when the Great-Grandfathers of the Ancestors were still children like you. In the shell pile, these bones and antlers have become very hard and make better tools than the bones of the fresh game that we eat. Sometimes we dig up the ancient bones to use and make tools to leave for our grandchildren's grandchildren. We bury them in shell mounds and the shells harden the bone, the way that fire hardens wood. Do you understand the lesson of the basket of shells, Grandson?'

"'By placing the shells close to where we live, Grandmother, I invited my brother the fly to come and feast, only I was the feast! By bringing the shells here, I kept the flies out of the village, so that they could feast far from the backs of us children. Also, Grandmother, I learned that all the people pile the shells in one place so that my great-great-great-granddaughter can have a strong needle made of bone to sew clothing for her grandchildren.

I learned that we pile the shells in one place so that my great-great-grandson can create a good tool for making a sharp knife from stone, using a hardened antler to shape it. I learned that Our People never waste anything and that we eat the sweet meat of these shells so that our grandchildren may live.'

"'It is good that you learn this lesson, Little Hawk,' Grandmother said. 'You should also know that each shell can be used in special ways.' I followed my grandmother to her wigwam. She opened a basket and showed me a rattle that had been made by stringing shells together. 'In this way, shells can become musical instruments,' she said. Then, she held the shell in her hands and she blew into it vibrating her lips, making a trumpeting sound. 'So we can even use the shells to call over a great distance.'

"Then, she gave me this very shell, which had been given to her by her father on a canoe trip he had made to visit the southern people, the way that I did when I was a little older."

"'Our Southern Brothers are gifted with the meat from this large shell. Once they eat the meat, they can use this shell as a musical instrument.'

"She blew into the shell like this."

Grandfather Little Hawk blew into the conch shell through a hole made at the tip. The sound was so loud and unexpected, that Seagull and Many Smiles jumped. Seagull could feel her heart racing in her chest. Then, Little Hawk cupped his hand over the opening of the conch and was able to change the tones and the volume.

"The first time I heard it, the sound made me jump, too. But the music of this shell continues to remind me that Our People do not waste."

The story ended. Dancing Rain looked at Seagull and Many Smiles. "Why do you think Little Hawk told that story just then?"

"Because you gave Grandfather the conch," Seagull guessed.

"I try to look into the hearts of those listening by feeling their energy and watching their eyes. Sometimes, I can tell that a group will be especially interested in the ocean, and then I might pass Little Hawk the shell. He will tell the story of his grandmother. Sometimes, I will see that this is a young group of people that may not have learned the lesson about wasting things and needs to be reminded, so I hand the shell to Little Hawk, and he tells the story. Sometimes, everyone looks a little sleepy, and by handing

Little Hawk the shell and encouraging him to tell the story, he will blow the shell and wake everyone up."

"So that's why you handed the conch to Grandfather," Seagull laughed, "because we were nodding off."

"Yes, children, because you are already awakened to the message, *we do not waste*. I know you both respect every part of the animals' gifts to us."

Dancing Rain continued the lesson.

"The job of the Caretaker is to communicate the need of the listeners to the Storyteller. Sometimes, the group we are telling a story to is very interested in music. Little Hawk's skill with the flute is especially well known. You have seen that people come from far away—from the land of the fires of the Northern Lights, from the land of the Bark Eaters, and beyond the mountains—to listen and learn from Little Hawk. And when the group is especially interested in music, I hand Little Hawk two flutes."

Many Smiles and Seagull exchanged excited glances. They both knew what story was coming. And if Dancing Rain had handed the flutes to *them*, they would both be able to tell this story, but they still would not be able to duplicate the feat that Little Hawk could accomplish at the end of the story.

Grandfather looked lovingly at the two flutes. He placed them on a blanket beside him and began the story quietly, inviting his listeners to lean toward him.

"It was another warm and sunny summer day," Little Hawk narrated. "I was practicing shooting my bow and arrow in the field, when I heard Grandfather's voice call me from the front of the wigwam."

"'Ey, Little Hawk, come over here.'"

When Little Hawk spoke like his grandfather, he always spoke in the same deep, gentle, wise tone of voice. Many Smiles and Seagull smiled fondly, because they knew this voice so well. Little Hawk used it only when he portrayed his grandfather. Seagull loved it because when she spoke to the ancestors, she could hear this very voice of her great-great-grandfather in the wind.

"So when Grandfather called me, I collected my arrows and I ran to see what he wanted.

"'Little Hawk, I want you to take a walk with me. We are going up on the hill,' my grandfather said.

"The hill was the South Mountain. It rose high up out of the valley. At the top was Crystal Lake, and it was so high up we could see for miles and miles all around. As we walked toward the foothill, Grandfather was telling me why we were going to the hill.

"'Little Hawk,' said Grandfather, 'we can learn lessons from animals of how to live in a good way. We must watch and listen to them when they speak to us in their way. We are going to sit among the trees and listen to their lesson for us today.'

"'Grandfather, you said *us*. You already know the good way to live.'

"'Yes, that's true,' Grandfather replied, 'but grown-ups have to be reminded every so often of how to live in a good way.'"

Little Hawk moved his body to pretend he was walking and, as he pantomimed walking, he looked up the way a young boy looks up at his grandfather. Seagull felt that if she could look carefully enough into her grandfather's eyes, she might be able to see the actual reflection of Little Hawk's grandfather.

Little Hawk continued. "We reached the brook, crossed it, and soon we were among trees in the foothills. We walked along on a narrow path; Grandfather walked ahead and I trailed right behind. He stooped to pick up a straight branch that had fallen from one of the trees. He used it as a walking stick. I found a walking stick, too. It was much smaller than Grandfather's stick, but I used it just as he did."

Here again, Little Hawk used actions to tell the story. He picked up and held an invisible walking stick, and seemed to lean the weight of his many years on the stick, walking carefully, understanding that the Grandfather Tree had dropped the stick so that he might use it. Then he was the boy Little Hawk, watching and repeating his grandfather's every move, exaggeratedly, comically, the way a young boy innocently and lovingly imitates his grandfather.

"Grandfather sat down and leaned back against a big tree with his legs stretched out. He motioned to me to come and sit next to him. I could understand everything he said to me even when he only used his hands. I sat down and leaned back against the same big tree with my legs stretched out, just like Grandfather."

How is it, Many Smiles wondered, *that Little Hawk can make me feel his grandfather's presence? Does he call his grandfather's spirit to help him tell the story? And how can it be that sometimes Little Hawk, without moving, can sit like a boy and then, in the next moment, can sit like his grandfather?*

"Grandfather's eyes were closed, so I closed mine. He was quiet, so I was quiet, too, and we sat that way for a little while.

"'I want you to listen to the birds,' Grandfather said. 'They have a message for you today. They are going to tell you how to live in a good way. Then you are going to tell me what the birds told you. You must be very quiet. Do not move around. Close your eyes and listen only to the birds.'

"'Only to the birds will I listen, Grandfather.'

"My grandfather closed his eyes again and so did I. Just then I heard leaves rustling close by. I opened my eyes and saw two chipmunks chasing each other, back and forth, over Grandfather's legs. I was so excited, I started laughing. The chipmunks stopped, looked up at me, and ran away just as fast they could—and that was really fast."

"'Grandfather, the chipmunks were playing tag across your legs and they made me laugh.'

"'Yes, Little Hawk, animals bring joy to us just as people bring joy to each other. Now, let us hear what the birds have to say.'

"Grandfather closed his eyes again and so did I. Just then I felt a tickling on my leg. I tried to keep my eyes closed, but I just had to see what was tickling me. I opened my eyes and saw an ant run up my leg as if it were the South Mountain itself. I pretended I was the North Wind, and blew a gentle breeze on the ant.

"'Grandfather, an ant climbed my leg and I felt like I was a mountain.'

"'Yes, Little Hawk, insects help us look at things more closely, just as all people we know, or who we are yet to meet, teach us to look at things more closely. Now, let us hear what the birds have to say.'

"Grandfather closed his eyes again and so did I. Just then I felt a breeze begin to grow and I noticed the smell of rain in the wind. I imagined the rain coming, and playing and splashing in puddles, and shouting back at the thunder.

"'Grandfather, I smelled the rain and the breeze, and I wondered what was to come.'

"'Yes, Little Hawk, paying attention to the wind helps us know what is to come, just like paying attention to the lives of all people, young and old, tell us about our own future and past. Now let us hear what the birds have to say.'

"Grandfather closed his eyes again and so did I."

Little Hawk continued the story. "'Grandfather, I will really listen,' I promised. I leaned back against the tree and closed my eyes, again listening for the birds. Something was scampering in the underbrush. Maybe it was our little friends, the chipmunks. I felt something tickling my leg. Maybe it was our little friend, the ant. I could hear something moving the tops of the trees. Maybe it was our friend, the breeze.

"That's when a bird started singing."

Little Hawk took the first flute and placed it to his mouth. He played a simple tune that he repeated seven times. With his eyes still closed, Little Hawk seemed to be listening to a sound above him.

"The bird's song seemed to be coming from the same tree we were leaning against. Its song was so bright and so clear that I knew it was singing its song just for me.

"Another bird started singing *its* song."

Grandfather Little Hawk took the second flute in his other hand. He played a different tune on the lower-toned flute, and repeated the melody seven times.

"The second bird's song was just as clear and bright as the bird singing above us."

Grandfather Little Hawk's voice was so excited, that Seagull forgot that Little Hawk was a Storyteller who had just played a tune on the flute. In her imagination, Seagull saw a little boy with his eyes closed smiling toward the sound of a bird.

"I opened my eyes very slowly to see the second bird. There it was on the bottom branch in the tree right in front of us—a beautiful, yellow, and black bird. When it stopped singing, the first bird in the tree above us started its song. When that bird stopped, the other started. Back and forth they sang, first one, then the other.

"Very slowly I moved my head back so I could see what the bird overhead looked like. It sat on the lowest branch right over our heads. Its red and white colors were as bright and happy as its song." The Storyteller leaned forward.

He spoke in a quiet voice. "The two birds did not look alike, one was really little and the other was big. One was black and yellow, the other red and white, and each had its own song. I closed my eyes again and listened as Grandfather told me to do.

"As soon as my eyes closed, I could hear both birds start singing their own songs at the same time."

Many Smiles noticed how Little Hawk opened his eyes and looked at the small flute, then at the larger flute. At this point, Little Hawk's listeners would always wonder, *which flute will he play?* He said that both birds *had started singing at the same time.* He put a small flute in his mouth, then the larger flute. At first, it looked as if he was going to give up on the idea of playing either flute, but this seeming dilemma was just part of the storytelling. His indecision about which flute to play was very funny. Many Smiles and Seagull always laughed, no matter how many times they heard the story.

The effect was truly dramatic—would Little Hawk be able to play the two flutes at the same time? He put one flute in his mouth, then the other, and finally put them both in his mouth, and played the two separate melodies at the same time! Many Smiles watched his teacher in awe. Many Smiles had tried to play both flutes together many times, but he had difficulty enough playing just one. Grandfather continued the story.

"It sounded like one beautiful, happy song the birds had been waiting to sing together for a long time. As I listened my heart became as happy as their song. They sang and sang and I listened and listened."

Once again, effortlessly, or so it seemed to his listeners, Grandfather Little Hawk was playing different tunes on two flutes at the same time, and they sounded beautiful together.

Then he spoke again. "When the birds stopped, it was at the same time and on the same note. Quickly I opened my eyes and watched the two birds fly away.

"Grandfather said the birds would tell me something that I must learn. What did they tell me? What did I learn? Now I must think. The birds were not the same colors. One had yellow and black feathers and the other was red and white. One was little and one was big. Each had its own song. And they had sung together.

"Then I knew what the bird's message was to me! They told me you don't have to be the same kind of bird to have a happy song. And you do not have to be or look exactly the same to come together and make one beautiful song.

"Grandfather opened his eyes, looked at me, and smiled. He stood up and said, 'You have been very quiet Little Hawk. It is in my quiet times that many answers to questions come to me. Have you had answers come to you?'

"We began to walk the narrow footpath back toward the village. I was quiet and so was Grandfather. We reached the brook and crossed it in silence. We arrived at our wigwam and Grandfather motioned to me with his hands to sit next to him.

"'What did the birds teach you about how to live in a good way?'

"I did not answer right away because I was still thinking. Then I told him of my message from the birds, but not only from the birds, from the chipmunks, from the ant, and from the breeze. He smiled, put his arm around my shoulders and gave me a big hug.

"'As you grow older, you may begin to forget the things you learned today. Always remember, take time to stop, to look, and listen to your forest friends. They never forget, and their messages about how to live in a good way are all around us—all the time.'"

Grandfather Little Hawk once again played the song of the two birds. Then he sang quietly, looking Seagull and then Many Smiles in the eye:

> *All around is the good way*
> *All around each day*
> *Hear the message*

Hear the message
Go in the good way.

"So you see," Grandmother Dancing Rain explained, "before we tell a story, we fill the space with our presence, and with our awareness. We notice who comes and where the people's attention is. We feed their attention. The job of the Caretaker is to understand the kind of attention that a group needs, and the lessons that could help the people to live in a good way. When I am the Caretaker, I focus on the way the audience calls to the Storyteller. The Storyteller must respond to lift The People to a new place, so they can learn the lessons of the ancestors.

"Each item I hand Little Hawk represents one specific story," Grandmother said, handing a small, decorated birchbark basket to Little Hawk.

Little Hawk smiled, stood, and showed the basket to his students.

"The sound of the drum," Little Hawk began, "was like a great heartbeat and the singing voices carried by the wind made me glad to be at the gathering of the Penobscot. They are a kind and welcoming people. At the gathering many people invited me to listen to their songs, watch them dance their dances, and taste their foods. As I walked around their village, I saw a grandmother working carefully making a birchbark basket. She was decorating the basket with shapes that represented flowers, trees, and other children of the Plant Nation. The quillwork was beautiful and the grandmother had repeated the same pattern along the whole border of her basket.

"She looked up at me with a big, warm smile," Little Hawk continued.

"'Hello, there.'" Little Hawk's voice gently imitated the feel of a grandmother.

"'Hello. Would you mind if I looked at what you are working on?'

"'Oh, no, child,' she said. 'Come around to this side of the basket and take a closer look.'" Many Smiles was amazed. Little Hawk's voice switched so easily from that of a grandmother to that of a child!

"I could now see that she was nearly finished with her design. The red-and-yellow flower design completely surrounded the white birch and repeated itself upside down, the way the water reflects the pattern of the flowers on the shore. It was crafted with such care! I noticed one dark-brown quill among all that beauty, and I thought, was it a mistake?

"'That brown quill looks like it doesn't belong there,' I said out loud.

"'Oh yes,' she said, 'it does belong there.'

"'Why would you stitch in a quill that looks so out of place in your beautiful work?'

"'I put it there,' she replied with that same warm smile on her face, 'to remind me.'

"'To remind you of what, Grandmother Basket Maker?'

"'To remind me not to think that I am better than other human beings. To remind me to learn from mistakes. I am not perfect. It reminds me that my triumphs belong to my teachers and my mistakes belong to me.'"

3.4 The Feeling Lesson:
A Short Lesson About the Call
and Response of Emotion

"Tonight, children, we are going to teach you a special lesson."

The eager students exchanged grins and Many Smiles noticed that Seagull's hair sparkled like the fire.

Grandfather Little Hawk unpacked a drum. He sat with his back turned to Grandmother, facing Seagull and Many Smiles. He kept a steady, slow beat. As the drum grew louder, Grandmother Dancing Rain looked tired, turned her eyes to the sky and danced sadly.

Many Smiles' grin vanished from his face. His heart was filled with pity for Dancing Rain, but he could not explain why. Grandmother's eyes filled with tears. Seagull started to get up to console Dancing Rain, but grandmother pointed to the ground as if to ask her to stay seated. Now her steps cried, her feet dragged, and she began to sing, "*Way—Hai—Yo!*" Her voice had the sound of loneliness. Her voice was like that of Many Smiles' mother the night he left her wigwam to learn to be a Storyteller.

"Sorrow," said Little Hawk.

Grandmother then took a rattle and put it in Little Hawk's hand. Grandfather played the same rhythm he had before.

Grandmother stumbled and tripped. Many Smiles gasped and Seagull struggled to her feet to save Grandmother from falling into the fire. But Grandmother had not lost her balance. She signaled Seagull to sit back down. She spun in the air like a bat following a windblown mosquito. Then she stuck out her tongue. Then she sang, "*Way—Hai—Yo!*"

Seagull and Many Smiles began to feel dizzy themselves. The dizzier they felt, the dizzier Dancing Rain became. Grandmother's stumbling steps, the tilt of her head, the sound of her voice, no one in the wigwam could resist. Many Smiles started laughing and Seagull laughed, too. Even Grandfather Little Hawk began to laugh, though he had seen none of what she had done.

"Silliness," he said. "You see? Each of us can convey emotion. A Storyteller must tell the truth, must *feel* the truth.

"The drumming is the people's heartbeat. Music in a story helps people know that they are free to feel, and that they can react. I was sitting with my back to Dancing Rain, but I was able to guess the emotion she was dancing. How did I know? I watched how you responded to her. One of the important things a Caretaker can do is understand how the story can make each person feel. The Caretaker can use music, or the light from the fire, or movement to guide the people to respond to the feeling of the story at that point."

"As the people feel our sorrow, our silliness, our laughter, and have responded with their own feelings, it helps them remember the lesson that the story teaches," Dancing Rain added.

"Now one of you be the heartbeat, and the other be the feeling. Take the emotion of sorrow. Dance it, and sing it."

Many Smiles took a shell rattle and Seagull moved in front of the fire. "At first, we will call out the emotion, and you will dance and sing it. Many Smiles, I ask you to keep a heartbeat rhythm with the rattle. Know that you are playing the rhythm of sorrow, but do nothing to change the beat." Many Smiles started the heartbeat. Seagull danced, danced sorrow. Grandmother stopped her.

"Right now, Granddaughter, you are only a *girl dancing* sorrow. Seagull, to dance sorrow you must forget that you are dancing. Close your eyes this time. Think of a moment when you *really* felt sad. Do not think of the story of that moment, just how you feel remembering that sad moment. Now send that feeling to the people. Look into their eyes and you will see that same feeling coming back to you. It's a very deep feeling in call and response. The audience will respond and understand of the measure of sorrow that is in your voice, your eyes, your hands and feet. Your message is for all of them, so give them all of you at that moment of sadness."

Grandmother spoke while Seagull danced. "Think of the strength in the words and the feeling they bring, a feeling they have had and can identify with you. When you speak softly and quietly you will feel that the people will also become quiet. Weave laughter throughout your storytelling. Reflect joy whenever joy is present. Do not let those moments escape you. Share joy fully. Fill the air with joy, as you shared sadness."

Many Smiles kept the rhythm on the rattle. He began to feel Little Hawk and Dancing Rain's sorrow as they watched Seagull dance with a sadness that could be seen, heard, and felt.

"That was good. To be able to identify with the people's feelings is very important. Once we were visiting another village and before the people had gathered, Little Hawk played the flutes to make the children laugh. During the story of Two Birds, he played with two flutes and the children found the joy in the two birds singing and laughter was their response. I learned that you can help guide behavior in a good way by using some very simple offerings, like a way of dancing, or the sound of a flute."

Many Smiles remembered times where the people had been quieted with a surprisingly unexpected beginning. Other times, when children jostled and even adults could barely contain their energy, Little Hawk would open the storytelling while sitting by the fire, playing calming flute music. Everyone would sit and become quiet.

In either case, both Dancing Rain and Little Hawk would begin by talking about their connection with their grandparents. In that way, the people got to know Little Hawk and Dancing Rain more closely, in a good way. Many Smiles noticed how very often Little Hawk would focus on a smiling face in the circle of listeners and smile back, responding with a warmth that helped to put everyone at ease.

Once the people were comfortable, the Storytellers could share many emotions, never forgetting to add a touch of humor.

When the mood became too heavy, or when the people had been sitting too long, the Storytellers would invite a few, and sometimes all, to participate, to dance, or to play a rattle, or to sing a response. Then everyone would feel they had personally contributed to the story.

As they learned from Grandfather Little Hawk and Grandmother Dancing Rain, Many Smiles and Seagull had started telling stories to The People in the village. They applied all they had learned. But they agreed that *something* was still missing. "When you tell the stories," Many Smiles said to Grandmother, "I notice that everyone leaves the storytelling with good thoughts and lessons that will benefit their lives in a good way. Seagull and I also tell stories that teach these good thoughts. But when you tell the stories, the people leave with something else, a feeling that is very deep and very good. I often wonder, what is at the root of this good feeling?"

Then Grandmother smiled and handed Seagull a rattle and Many Smiles a drum.

"Play love," she said.

Many Smiles found this the easiest and the most difficult of all the tasks. He found a place in himself, a very young place, and he loved the child that was alive in him. He loved Seagull, and everyone in the wigwam, and this clan, and his own clan, but he still had to keep the same rhythm as Seagull. When he lost himself in his feelings, he would lose awareness of Seagull's rattle, yet his spirit stayed attached to the rhythm.

Grandmother allowed the drumming to continue. Many Smiles began to focus on the drum itself. This drum had been made by Dancing Rain's mother. It had a beautiful sound. Many Smiles had watched drums being made, watched how the wet deerskin tightened as it dried, creating a wonderful, tough skin over the wooden hoop. He had seen hoops cut from fallen trees, split with wedges, sliced by stone knives, softened over fire, and bound into circles. He remembered his old name, which now belonged to the storm. Without the drum, what would he have been named as a child? Many Smiles drummed for love of the drum and for love of drumming. His heartbeat matched the heartbeat of Seagull's rattle.

"If you want the people to leave with this deep and special feeling, Grandson Many Smiles," Grandmother Dancing Rain's soft voice blended with the rhythm, "remember to fill the space with love and embrace the people's hearts so they can respond with love."

Meanwhile, Seagull's rattle sounded in a heartbeat rhythm as she listened to the sounds of love in the air, children playing outdoors in the rain, dogs barking. She smelled the smoky scent of dried fish, the smell of the birchbark of a brand-new wigwam, the smell of things familiar, the heads of the little ones, the fire, the first summer berries, the pemmican, the teas, and the stews. And Seagull listened again to the heartbeat. She knew that no matter how far away she was from her people, that love would not change. This thought filled her with a great joy and she burst into song at the very instant Many Smiles also burst into song.

Her song was very much like his. Both songs ended abruptly, as soon as they each remembered that they were singing. Dancing Rain looked at Little Hawk and their eyes shared a secret knowing laugh, which though silent, echoed from the Storytellers to the people and back.

3.5 An Eastern-Facing Story: Anticipation and Awareness

One night, on a bluff that overlooked the Great Water, Grandfather Little Hawk told his village an Eastern-Facing story. He began the story when the Sun was already sitting in the highest branches of the trees to the west. As the light disappeared from the sky, wind, fire, and waves all seemed to move with his story. When Little Hawk opened his arms wide, it seemed the breezes would pick up. When his story grew quiet, it seemed the winds would grow quiet as well. As Many Smiles stood at the edge of the gathering, he felt awed, and maybe a little bit sad. *How can I ever hope to be a great Storyteller if I can't move the breeze?*

Little Hawk told his story to the Setting Sun, and the story ended as darkness fell over the Great Waters. His voice summoned the night creatures into the sky. Then, he began to sing the stars into place in the sky. He lifted his hands to a patch of darkening blue and sang. A star appeared, and then another!

As Grandfather Little Hawk called the stars into the sky, his body swayed back and, immediately, a breeze began to blow. Now, he played his drum and the heartbeat of the drum called more stars into the sky, one by one. He began to dance slowly, lifting the drum toward the sky and then bending toward the earth. Soon everyone was standing, dancing with Little Hawk around the fire. Seagull stood next to Many Smiles. She whispered, "Did you see him pick up the drum? Weren't his hands just empty?" Many Smiles' eyes grew wide. It was true! His hands were empty!

But how, how, and how? Too many lessons here! Little Hawk sang into the fire and the fire responded by producing a fireball that flared and then disappeared. Little Hawk directed the fire into the sky by dancing and drumming. Above the circle of listeners, a bright, new star shone. Many Smiles felt he could never call the stars into the sky or make the wind dance by telling a story. Seagull had seen the Eastern-Facing story many times, but now she, too, wondered how she was ever going to tell this story. And yet, somehow they would learn, just as their grandfathers' grandfathers had learned to do the same. Later that night, Seagull and Many Smiles sat in the wigwam of Little Hawk and Dancing Rain.

"You want me to tell you the story of how I learned?" Grandfather leaned against his backrest. "What can I tell you? I cannot teach you this skill." Many Smiles felt his heart sink like a stone weight on a fishing net. Little Hawk smiled. "But I have asked someone who can teach you to come for a visit."

"Who?" Seagull asked.

"Many Smiles' Grandfather, Deer Cloud. As you know, Seagull, your father, Howling Wolf, was asked to Many Smiles' village earlier this week. I knew that both of you would see the Eastern-Facing story, and I knew you would want to learn how to tell it, so I asked Howling Wolf to invite Many Smiles' Grandfather, Deer Cloud, to visit us. Howling Wolf told me that Deer Cloud has accepted my invitation and will be here around sundown tomorrow. I have invited him to hear Many Smiles tell a story."

Many Smiles leaped to his feet. The small fire in the wigwam danced and flared as he began to pace. "But I *have* no story to tell!"

Little Hawk raised his hands gently, palms up, and smiled. "Grandson, you're worrying the fire. See how it responds to the way you're feeling." He turned to Seagull. "Calm the fire, Granddaughter."

"But, I've had no time to prepare. What am I going to do?" Many Smiles continued to pace. Seagull moved her body to block the fire from Many Smiles. It still hopped and sputtered.

"Calm the fire, Granddaughter," Grandfather said again.

"But how can I calm the fire with Many Smiles pacing about?" Dancing Rain looked at Little Hawk and smiled. Little Hawk reclined some more and breathed a contented sigh.

"You can't calm the fire while Many Smiles is nervous and pacing as he is."

Seagull cast an irritated glance at Many Smiles. "If I tell him to calm down, he will obey for a little while and then he'll grow nervous again, and the fire will jump and sputter. The room is filled with an unusual energy. Many Smiles is nervous, the fire is irritated, and Grandmother and Grandfather are calm. And I'm feeling like the fire. I'm irritated by Many Smiles' nervousness. Am I the fire? If so, what can I do to calm my irritation?"

She looked at Grandfather and Grandmother, who were watching her, lovingly. She leaned toward the fire.

"Oh Fire, Grandmother looks at Grandfather with her deep understanding. I can't calm your nervousness. I have failed, and still Grandfather and Grandmother look at me with love. Fire, even though you will not calm down, I look at you lovingly.

"Once, a grandfather traveled a long way to hear his grandson tell a story. And when the grandson told his story, the grandfather looked at his grandson with deep understanding. The grandson had no fear. He remembered that storytelling is play and that he had very, very often played in front of his grandfather. His grandfather had always watched him play lovingly, and with deep understanding, for that is the way of grandparents."

Many Smiles stopped pacing and sat down beside Seagull. He fingered the pouch with the storytelling stone. "Fire," Many Smiles said, "please do not be disturbed by my nervousness. Here, in this wigwam, we look on you as we look on each other, with love and respect, as Seagull has said. We are all calm."

Dancing Rain took a piece of cedar off the fire. She unrolled a blanket and took out a stone knife. Expertly, she scraped the charcoal off the stick, and gathered the powder on a square of deerskin. Once the stick had been carved, she held up the deerskin full of powdered charcoal and passed the skin to Little Hawk.

"The night sky was clear, and Seagull had been asked to calm the fire. She filled the room with love, and the fire grew calm, and the stars twinkled in the sky above," Dancing Rain said. All of a sudden, the fire twinkled with thousands of tiny sparks. Many Smiles watched Little Hawk blow the powdered charcoal onto the fire to produce the sparks. It reminded him of the fireball he'd seen at the evening storytelling.

"Grandmother, it was you! You blew something on the fire to make the fireball. Did you also hand Grandfather Little Hawk the drum? We didn't even notice. It seemed one moment Grandfather's hands were empty, and the next he had a drum."

Grandmother smiled. "Pine burns swiftly with a quick light. Oak produces heat, but not much light. Ash produces heat and light. A good Caretaker knows how and when to feed the fire. Do the elders feel cold? Has the wigwam grown too hot? She knows when the time has come to let the fire go down.

"A Caretaker makes sure that the Storyteller uses the right amount of curiosity and laughter with surprise and tenderness. She watches the audience for the Storyteller. Are they restless? Disinterested? What do they consider funny?

"You, Seagull, and you, Many Smiles, will caretake each others' stories. You will make yourselves unnoticed and sit near the fire. You will play with fire until you know how to blow flour or charcoal onto the fire to create fireballs and sparks. You will blow downy seeds into the air. People will think it's snowing. You will put soft, crumbly wood in the fire to create smoke when it is needed. As a Caretaker, I felt that the people wanted to dance when Little Hawk summoned the stars. They wanted to greet the stars and summon a star themselves. That's why I handed Little Hawk the Dancing Drum. That told him that I felt that the people were ready to dance."

Many Smiles frowned. "I'm still worried about tomorrow. What sort of story will I tell my grandfather? And will he really teach me how to call the wind and the stars to come?"

Little Hawk stood and unrolled his sleeping blanket. "You carry too heavy a burden, Grandson. Now sleep."

Early the next morning, while the mosquitoes were still biting and the Sun was mostly a promise in the sky, Many Smiles went to the river to bathe. When he returned to the wigwam, Grandmother was already boiling seal bone and scraping fat off the surface of its hide to flavor the food Many Smiles and Seagull set out to gather. Grandmother sang as she prepared the seal. This was very important and sacred because the spirit of the seal had to be reassured that its bones and fat were used to a good purpose, and nothing was to be wasted.

What a feast they were going to have! Many Smiles especially loved the chewy, purple dulse that grew among the rocks in the north. His grandfather shared his taste for this seaweed. Soon Many Smiles and Seagull had gathered three baskets each of the choicest seafood. When they returned to the wigwam, they noticed that Little Hawk had roasted cattail pollen on a rock and had transferred most of the pollen into one of the storytelling bags.

The morning activity made the time pass quickly for Seagull. But to Many Smiles, the Sun was creeping slowly as a stealthy spider on a hot summer day. "What story will I tell my grandfather?" he asked Seagull.

Seagull smiled. "I know Grandfather Little Hawk and Grandmother Dancing Rain. I'm sure they have something in mind. But maybe you can think of a funny incident you remember and add it into a story."

Many Smiles shrugged. "I know a good lesson for a story, but I don't know the story yet."

"And what's the lesson?"

"Waiting for something you wish for makes the day seem to take a lot longer."

That afternoon, Seagull and Many Smiles put on their most elaborately decorated clothing. They oiled their skin and hair with seal oil, and sat on a cattail mat, playing with their story pebbles. Each time a slight disturbance came from the path beyond the water, Many Smiles would run to see if his grandfather had arrived.

The first time he heard the hawk cry and the blue jay call, he ran to the middle of the path, but it was only Gray Dog, Seagull's mother, returning from gathering medicine from the sea. Many Smiles helped her carry the medicines to her home.

The second time he heard a dog bark from the direction of the stream, it was only Sea Mink, an older boy, who'd been playing in the stream and had hurt his knee on a river rock. Many Smiles carried him to the hut of the Puoin. The third and fourth time, two of the village grandmothers had gone to the river to fetch water. Many Smiles helped them both carry the water back to their wigwams. The second grandmother had heard that Many Smiles' grandfather was coming and offered some maple candy because she had grown up in the same village with Grandfather.

He returned to the spot where Seagull was still playing with her pebble. "My grandfather is never going to get here," he sighed. "It seems like the whole village is crossing the stream today."

Still, his awareness was aimed keenly at the stream. He arrived at the stream in time to help a family of fishermen return with their catch. They thanked him and promised they'd ask the Chief to distribute extra meat to Little Hawk's wigwam in honor of Many Smiles' grandfather. A bear splashed through the stream around sunset, a salmon wriggling in its mouth.

Finally, the shadows of the trees were long and fading. "Grandfather," Many Smiles whispered, "it's time to come. Please come and be with me before the day gets too dark." Just as he heard the sounds of the night growing quiet around the stream, something startled the nightbirds. Many Smiles ran out to the path and tore toward the stream.

"Grandfather! Grandfather!" Grandfather waded though the stream and hugged his grandson.

"Oh, my Grandson, how you've grown!" Then he touched Many Smiles' hair. "I see your hair is still long."

Many Smiles laughed. "Grandfather, my hair will be long for many more years. I haven't even led my first moose hunt. It will be years before I marry." Many Smiles held his grandfather's hand and led him into the village. They walked in silence. In the open doorways of the many wigwams, small fires glowed. In the Chief's home, families met to collect their portion of the food gathered that day.

Seagull was returning with three baskets of food. "Many people wanted us to have extra food tonight," Seagull beamed. "The Chief gave us enough dulse to last for two weeks. The Chief was very pleased with you. He told me that many people of the village had good things to say about the way you helped them today, Many Smiles."

Grandfather looked proudly at his grandson. "Perhaps while we eat, you can tell me the story of what you did today."

Many Smiles beamed. How could he have forgotten? All the stories that ever were have already been told...told by the rocks to the trees, told by the trees to the animals, and told by the animals to The People. Why had he doubted that he'd have a good story to tell his grandfather when life itself was a great story!

"I must go down to the stream," Many Smiles said. He ran down toward the stream. He took off his moccasins and stepped into the water. He lifted the water to his lips. "Thank you, Stream, and thank you Creatures of the Day and Night for letting me know when someone was crossing the stream. You gave me the opportunity to help my people, and you gave me a story to tell."

As Many Smiles left the stream, his grandfather and Little Hawk approached him, walking through the tall grass towards the stream.

"Grandson, how did you know I was coming?" Grandfather asked.

"Grandfather Little Hawk told me."

"And how did you know when to meet me at the river?"

"Grandfather, I paid attention to every little sound along the stream. Every time I thought I heard something, I ran down to the stream. I was so anxious to see you that all I could focus on was the stream that I knew you'd be crossing."

Little Hawk laid a hand on Many Smiles' shoulder. "But what about dinner? What about getting the feast ready for your grandfather?"

Many Smiles shook his head. "I'm sorry, Grandfather. I just, well, I just knew that Seagull would take care of that. Maybe I took advantage."

Little Hawk shook his head. "She was happy to do that for you, as you would have been happy to do the same for her if the situation were reversed. You trusted her to take care of things and you felt that you were free to listen for your grandfather."

"Is that all right, Grandfather Little Hawk? Should I have paid more attention to preparing the feast?"

"Grandson, when you feel the same anticipation that you felt about seeing your grandfather, about greeting the wind or welcoming the night, then you will be able to call a breeze to you, and to call the stars into the sky.

"When I tell an Eastern-Facing story, I am so excited to welcome the breeze, that I look for signs of its coming in the movement of faraway trees and the movement of the plants and animals. It comes, and I rejoice! But since I am waiting so excitedly for it, I feel it before my listeners do. I know the habits of the breeze because I love it and wait for it. And I know that while I wait for the breeze, Grandmother Dancing Rain will pay attention and take care of all the people watching me.

"Tomorrow, before sunrise, you and Dancing Rain should go to stand above the Great Water. Tell her that the Sun and the wind are coming. Tend a fire for her and let her wait for them as if they were beloved relatives, the way you waited for your grandfather today. You will see that a Storyteller does not call the breeze. He does not bring the stars into the sky, he invites the breeze and the waves and the stars. Then he waits for them and welcomes them. And while he waits, his Caretaker tends the fire."

That night, Many Smiles told the story about waiting for his grandfather. He moved and jumped up and pretended to be the Puoin, the injured boy, the grandmothers, the fishermen, and the bear. And as he reached the end of the story, he realized that he had lost the point of the story and he feared that the story would end in failure. Seagull looked at Many Smiles, and understood what she needed to do. She unwrapped the stick that Grandmother Dancing Rain had carved the night before from the fire she had calmed. As Many Smiles moved forward toward his listeners, Seagull slipped the stick into his hand. The stick reminded him of the fact that he was loved. He looked at the stick, and sighed and smiled.

"Today I learned that waiting for something you love makes the Sun seem to move more slowly in the sky. We cannot make the waiting move faster, but we can fill that long waiting with love. If we do that, unexpected things will come to us.

"I have also learned that those who love me want me to tell a good story. I shouldn't fear their judgment. Grandparents, I thank you for listening to my story with love. You see me like no one else."

Many Smiles caught a glimpse of Seagull's dark eyes shining in the firelight. He passed the stick back to her. "You are all related to the great movement of my days. I look forward to the things I can do for my people as I wait for the next important part of my life. I tell the Eastern-Facing story of my life and I love it into existence, trusting..." he looked at Seagull, "trusting that my Caretaker will tend the fire."

Grandfather smiled and lit his pipe. "This is a very good story, my grandson. Little Hawk and Dancing Rain have taught you well, and Seagull has tended your fire very well. Now, Many Smiles, I must tell you that your uncle, Becomes Unseen, has asked you to come back with us and to hunt the first moose of the season."

Many Smiles felt a joy that startled his throat and filled his eyes, so that he had to look skyward and let the tears of joy flow.

"So I will become a man!"

"Yes, Grandson. The District Chief will visit in the spring. We want you to sit on the council when the Great Decision is made."

"I will be glad when you are a man, Many Smiles," Seagull said quietly.

The next morning, before sunrise, Many Smiles woke Seagull and they walked to the land above the Great Water. Many Smiles made a fire. "Seagull," Many Smiles said, "the Sun and the morning wind are coming. Wait for them as if they were your beloved relatives, the way I waited for my grandfather."

"As I will wait for you to return in the springtime," Seagull said.

"It seems that sometimes all we do is wait," Many Smiles said.

"I think that's what makes a good story. A good story sometimes keeps feeding you questions and then waits until life teaches you the answer. Sometimes if you get answers too easily, you don't value the lesson as much."

A smile dawned across the faces of Many Smiles and Seagull at the same instant. Finally, they had learned the lesson of the story of Little Hawk's Grandfather and the Great Fish.

Seagull sat by the fire and pretended to play with her story heart in its leather pouch. Then she jumped up and ran to the edge of the land, lifted her hands and beckoned to the sky. The breeze started to blow. Many Smiles added fuel to the fire and watched. Seagull lowered her head, put her hands into the sand, and then slowly began to stand. As she did, she lifted a thin light into the sky. She called a morning breeze to dance across the fire, and then she faced east once more, and pulled the light even higher into the sky. She pretended that the Sun was a large fish she had speared and was pulling to land.

She greeted it like a hungry fish hunter, grateful for the feast it would provide her people.

Seagull danced on the breeze like a...like a *seagull*. Her body hovered, but her arms moved like wings balancing her so she wouldn't fly off. Then, from the lowlands, the seagulls did come, two, now three, and they perched on the edge of the land and watched Seagull dance the Sun into the air. "Akakakakak!" Sang Seagull and Many Smiles. The seagulls threw their beaks towards the sky and sang a greeting to the Sun.

3.6 Our Many Children:
Changing Voices

Now it is the wintertime, and Many Smiles has gone back to the village of Grandfather Deer Cloud and Uncle Becomes Unseen. While we wait for winter to pass, let me tell you how I think toys first came into the world.

At the time of the First Storytelling, Grandmother Rock told all her tales to First Child, and First Child told the stories to The People. But as First Child grew, the urge to teach these stories and pass them on also grew.

First Child offered the stories to the Elders.

"Ah, First Child," the Elders all said, "we would love to learn these stories and be able to tell them. And yet we are busy making all the important decisions. We are busy teaching the younger people of our tribe. Since the world is so new, we have many tasks to complete so that our descendants may live in a good way."

The younger adults of the tribe were happy to learn the stories, but they had to feed their families, and watch the little ones, and help the elders, and since the world was new, they had so many duties that they did not have time to learn the stories. But they encouraged First Child to teach all the children the stories. So First Child gathered the children together, not just the children of the Two-Legged Nation, but also the children of the Four-Leggeds and the Winged Nation.

"I will give you each a storytelling stone," said First Child, "and I will teach you every story."

The bears quickly learned the stories of the great wrestling matches. The wolves loved the stories about waking the Moon. The birds liked to sing their stories. The bobcat loved to tell stories about the hunt. Even the shy baby moose and deer learned stories. They loved the stories of dancing.

First Child taught each animal the type of story that interested it the most, until all the stories that Grandmother Rock had taught First Child could be repeated by at least one animal. Then came disaster. Since this was the first year ever on Mother Earth, no one realized that winter was coming. When the cold came, most of the furry animals grew too tired to learn and some fell into a deep sleep. The birds wanted to fly to warmer places. First Child told the animals that if this cold ever ended, they should all return to learn more stories. In the meantime, all the young animals should practice by playing their favorite games.

The Two-Leggeds felt very disappointed. Unlike the other animals, they couldn't decide which were their favorite games.

"Well," said a child named Standing Heron, "we like to wrestle—"

"—like the bear," said the bear cub. "Humans wrestle, and hunt fish, and now that it's cold, I've even seen some of them dressed in bear coats."

"But we also like to dance," said a girl named Spotted Shorttail.

"Like the deer," said the fawn. "Humans dance on long legs, and they like to leap. And often, I have seen them wear our thin coats."

"But also we love to sing and sit on branches," said a boy named Jumping Dog.

"Like us birds," said three ravens, speaking all at once. All the animals gave the humans advice on how they should play. Through the long, cold season, the human children wondered which animal's advice to take. Then came the spring, and it was a most welcome surprise. But the winter had left a long wall of ice and had carved new rivers in the brand-new land. Much of the land was carried off by melting streams. The human children were cut off from the other creatures and from First Child.

The children didn't know what to do, but Spotted Shorttail, who was a clever girl, suggested that they pretend that they were back with First Child learning all the stories. They all took their storytelling pebbles. One had a pouch for his stone made of bearskin. He took some more bearskin, and made a tiny bear cub. Another made a bird of feathers and sticks, and yet another made a tiny version of First Child out of clay. When all the animals were made, they played a game where First Child was teaching them all the stories.

Then Glooscap, who saw how hard these children had worked, sent spirits to these little creatures they'd created so that as long as the children played with them, the children would be able to hear them and move them as if they were real. The children would be able to feel these tiny spirits, but no adult would, unless that adult could keep that spirit of childish play alive.

And this is how toys came into the world. Each original toy, because it was made from one of the storytelling stones, knew the stories of Grandmother Rock, and could tell stories to the human children, as long as they listened. The children played and spoke in the high, quick, beautiful voice of the bird, or the gruff, low, stutter of the moose, or the deep music of the bear. The children learned to speak with all the voices of the forest, and used all the voices in their play.

In the spring, Many Smiles returned to the wigwam of Little Hawk and

Dancing Rain as a man. At the welcome meal, Little Hawk had told the story of how toys came into being.

"Speaking with the voices of the forest, using all your voices in your play—this is something that a Storyteller must do, my grandchildren. Dancing Rain and I have been busy all winter. We have made you a gift." Little Hawk beckoned to the young Storytellers, and as they watched, he unrolled a cattail mat. Inside were all sorts of small dolls, a bear, a wolf, an otter, various birds, a moose, a chipmunk, a beaver, a whale, a turtle, a snake—the whole collection was wonderful.

"Thank you, Grandmother, Grandfather!"

Dancing Rain smiled and raised her hand. "No, please do not thank us. Instead, let these animals thank us." She spread the animals on the cattail mat. "Look at one of the animals. We'll turn our backs. Now, when you decide on one, thank us in the voice of that creature. We will have to decide which creature you chose. Remember, use your voice only. For this game, try not to use your body, since that will sometimes give it away." Seagull looked at Many Smiles. She stepped in front of Grandfather, Grandmother, and Many Smiles. She nodded, and tightened her throat, and spoke through puffy cheeks, sounding like a woman who had seen a great many years and a great many feasts.

"Oh, oh, oh, thank you, thank you. Thank you so much, Grandfather Little Hawk, and, and oh, thank you Grandmother Dancing Rain. Oh, oh, how very nice. Thank you, thank you."

"Walrus?" Dancing Rain guessed.

Little Hawk nodded. "I agree."

"Now let's do some call and response," Dancing Rain suggested. "Each of you choose an animal. I will call with the voice and the personality and the spirit of the animal I choose, and you will all respond with the voice, the personality, and the spirit of the animal you choose, but do not touch the animal you choose." Grandmother called, the other three responded, but no one could guess any of the animals the younger Storytellers had chosen.

"Alright, we'll sit with our backs to each other, so that none of us can see what the other one has chosen. When I call, you touch the animal you choose, and you make it move, and dance and respond. No one is to look at what anyone else is doing."

This time Seagull and Many Smiles were successful.

"See the difference touching makes! Make the animal dance, see it dance and be its voice and movement while you forget that you are the Storyteller.

"This is just what a child at play does. The sound might not even be the proper sound the animal makes, but these dolls, they will give you their special voices, and they will change what you say and how you tell a story. Now we will repeat the story of First Child and the Animals in the voices of two squirrels."

Squirrel's story of First Child and the Animals

Our Many, Many, Many Children

"Oh you Two-Leggeds whose bushy tails grow out of the back of your heads, listen to me! There was once a time…"

"Once a time? There is always a time! It's now."

"Yes, but now *I'm* telling a story."

"So tell."

"Um, before squirrels lived in trees, before trees were big enough for us to jump into…"

"Was that before the time of nuts?"

"Yes, yes before the time of nuts."

"Then I'll tell the story. *Before the trees were big enough to grow nuts, there lived some very hungry squirrels.*"

"Would you please let *me* tell the story?"

"You don't need my permission. I'm just chasing your story."

"Oh. Are we having fun?"

"Of course. We're squirrels. We're also breathing. It's what we do. Please go on."

"Um…I forgot what I was going to say."

"Doesn't matter. Want to play tag?"

"Of course!"

And how would the Luna Moth tell this story?

Luna Moth's Story of First Child and the Animals

"One night I fluttered past the top of a wigwam where the birchbark walls glowed. I fluttered on a warm breeze made by a fire. At dusk I flitted, but by day I hid myself against the trunk of a sycamore tree, and I listened. I heard a story, and I will tell it to you, Grandmother Moon. I listened, and I watched, but felt sad because as First Child gave a stone to all the Storytellers, I knew that I was made of moonlight and my wings were thinner than a layer of paper birch. I couldn't possibly carry a stone. I visited my friend, the wolf, who is a daughter of the Moon just like I am. Just as the Moon taught me to dance upon the invisible wind, the Moon taught the wolf to sing. Wolf suggested that I talk to Grandmother Rock and ask her how I could carry a stone and become a Storyteller like the other creatures.

"When I landed on Grandmother Rock, she could barely hear my voice, so I asked the Moon to tell her what I desired. How could I carry a dark, round pebble like those other creatures? I awaited her answer.

"'Luna Moth, your wings are green and glowing and you are a faithful daughter of the Moon. You fly at night. In the dark where few can see you, you are so silent that you cannot be heard. So how could you be a Storyteller? Still, I have a very important job for you to do. I will teach you to be a Caretaker, so you will stay close to the fire of the Storyteller and cast shadows in your flight. Whenever a Storyteller sees you, you will remind the Storyteller that the stories come from the pebbles that are part of First Rock.'

"'But my voice is so small, how will the Storytellers hear me?'

"'I will ask the Moon to paint a picture of a pebble on each of your wings, one for the Storyteller, and one for the Caretaker. And because you are a good listener, I will give you a special gift. You will be able to hear the dreams of the creatures who sleep and you will tell their dreams to the Moon. Now, whenever you visit a wigwam, The People will know that the dreams they dream on the night of your visit have a very special Caretaker. You will be welcomed as a friend in the wigwam of every Caretaker as a sign that Grandmother Moon is listening to their dreams, and that they should pay special attention.'

"And I, the Luna Moth was happy, because even though I was too weak to carry a stone of my own, my job was special, and I learned that my weakness only meant that I had a different sort of strength."

"But that's exactly like the Turtle Story!" said Many Smiles.

"As told by Luna Moth. Yes, I switched animals. And I could have used the voices of other animals, the way I do in the Turtle Story."

"Please, Grandfather, tell us *that* story!"

And so he did.

How The Turtle Got His Shell

Long, long ago…

It was so long ago that there were no people. Only animals were living on Mother Earth, and Turtle did not have a shell.

Turtle lived beside a large river. The river was very wide and very deep and flowed very fast. Out in the middle of the river was a large island. Turtle lived in a little house made of earth and shells on the banks of the river.

Each day Turtle would wake up, stretch, and go down to the river and sit on his favorite rock and reach into the water and pick up shells. Then he'd wash them off and set them on the side. And, as he was doing this, he would look into the forest and then up into the sky. This day, Turtle looked into the sky and he saw Eagle. Eagle was circling high above and calling down to all the animals.

"It's a beautiful day in the forest!"

Turtle looked up at Eagle and Turtle started to cry.

"I don't want to be a turtle. I want to be an eagle. That way, I could call down to all the animals in the forest and tell them it's going to be a nice day."

Turtle picked up the shells he had cleaned, walked back to his house on the banks of the river, went inside, and carefully patted and pushed the shells into the floor and into the ceiling. After working on his house, he went to sleep.

The very next day, Turtle came out of his house, went to his favorite rock and sat on it. He reached into the water, picked up shells, cleaned them off, and looked into the forest. This day, Turtle saw Moose.

And Moose, with his large antlers scratched the trunk of the tree. The tree began to sway back and forth, back and forth. As the tree moved, the fruit on the branches fell to the ground. Well, when they saw this, the animals scampered to the base of the tree, picked up the fruits, and ran home to feed their families.

When Turtle saw this, he cried and complained again.

"I don't want to be a turtle anymore. I want to be a moose. That way, I can shake the trees and food will fall down for the animals and they can take the food home to feed their families."

Turtle picked up his shells, went home and again put them into the floor and into the ceiling. Then he went to sleep.

The next morning, Turtle woke up, went back to his favorite rock, and sat on it. He picked shells out of the water, washed them off, and put them on the side. Then he looked into the forest.

This day, when Turtle looked into the forest, Turtle saw Bear and Bear was growling very loud.

"GRRRRR!!!"

Turtle stood on tiptoe to see what all the loud growling was about. He saw that Bear was scolding big Raccoon who was picking on little Squirrel.

Bear was telling Raccoon, "We don't allow bullies in the forest. We must all live together in harmony, in a good way. Now, no more picking on Squirrel. Do you understand?"

"We understand," said Raccoon and Squirrel.

"Then go off into the forest, and live in harmony."

Raccoon and Squirrel scampered off into the forest.

Well, when Turtle saw that, Turtle said, "I don't want to be a turtle anymore. I want to be a bear. That way I can stop the big ones from picking on the little ones. And there won't be any bullying going on."

Turtle picked up his shells, went home, and again pressed them into the floor and into the ceiling. Then he went to bed.

The next morning at sunrise, Turtle heard screaming and hollering outside his house.

(Little Hawk used incredible skill until his face was contorted and his voice sounded exactly the way Many Smiles and Seagull imagined the tiny animals would speak.)

"Help! Help! Help! HELP!"

Turtle put his head outside the door and saw all the animals of the forest running down to the water, jumping into the river, and swimming out to the large island in the middle of the river. Turtle wanted to know why all the animals were running.

Turtle tried to stop Bear, but Bear went by very fast and did not stop. Turtle tried to talk to Moose, but Moose went by very fast and did not stop. None of the animals of the forest would stop to listen to Turtle's question.

Just then, Turtle looked up into the sky, and when he did, he saw Eagle. And Eagle was calling down, "Everyone run! Everyone run! Forest fire! Forest fire! Swim out to the island!"

Turtle had never been in a forest fire, but he had heard about them from the older animals and he was very, very frightened. He ran back into his house to hide. Just then a huge tree branch over his home fell down and squeezed Turtle in his house so tightly that he could hardly move or breathe. He gasped for air.

Turtle said, "I must get out of here or I'll burn up in the fire."

Turtle took his two front feet and pushed them outside the door. Then he took his two back feet and pushed them outside the door. He pulled and pushed, but he couldn't budge. So Turtle took a big, deep breath and put all of his strength into it. And he pulled and pushed so hard that he popped out. And when he popped out of his house, all the shells that he had collected and put on the floor and on the ceiling of his house were now squished to his stomach and to his back.

He ran down to the river's edge and was getting ready to jump in to swim out to the island to save himself from the fire, when he heard the voices of tiny animals crying for help.

(Little Hawk mimicked the tiny voices screaming and crying, but with very comic effect.)

"Help! Help! Please help! Turtle, help! Help us, please! The water is too deep and flows too fast. We are too little and we will all drown or burn in the fire. Please, Turtle, help us!"

"But…but…what can I do? I am only a little turtle. I…I…wait, look! I have a shell now! Everyone, climb up on my back. Quickly!"

So the little animals, the ants, the caterpillars, the grasshoppers, the crickets…all climbed onto Turtle's back.

Turtle swam out to the island. He let the animals off on the island and went back and picked up more of the little ones. Back and forth Turtle went carrying them to the island. On the last trip, the fire was very close to the water, but Turtle was able to save all the little ones.

Turtle was very tired. When he reached the island, he collapsed. A few moments later, he woke up to the sounds of all the animals shouting.

"A-Ho for Turtle! A-Ho for Turtle!"

Well, Turtle stood up and asked, "What is all this A-Ho for Turtle?"

The first one to come over to Turtle was Eagle, and Eagle said, "Turtle, you are a hero."

Turtle said, "Me, a little turtle? A hero?"

Eagle, said, "Yes, Turtle, you are a hero."

The next animal to come over was Moose, and Moose said, "Yes, Turtle, Eagle is right. You are a hero!"

Turtle smiled and began to like the sound of being called a hero.

The next to come over was Bear, and Bear said, "Turtle, you are a hero today! You made us all remember our first lesson—the big ones must always look after the little ones first. But we only thought about ourselves and did not care what happened to the little ones. We ran to the river, jumped in and swam out to the island. You, Turtle, remembered the little ones. And Turtle, you don't ever have to wish to be anyone except who you are. Continue to do good things, and share, and you'll always be a hero."

And, that's how Turtle got his shell.

Over the next several weeks, Many Smiles and Seagull created more dolls to represent different people they knew, stories they had heard, and new characters that they could play with. Some had green, pine needle hair, some had hair the color of dried grasses, and some had hair the color of shredded cedar bark.

"These are not the only creatures you can make," said Little Hawk. "I have traveled far and I have seen creatures carved out of sticks and whale-bone, or cut from cedar, or even folded out of birchbark that has been boiled soft and molded. I have even heard of far-off tribes who make dolls of clay that can be played like flutes. Pine cones also make wonderful bodies for creatures." He demonstrated, placing four sticks for legs into the scales of the pine cone, inserting another stick for the neck, and placing a smaller pine cone on the neck for the head. "I have made a deer!" he said. "You can do anything, use acorns, maple keys, hide."

Over the next moon, Many Smiles began to notice all the things that Dancing Rain could do with her voice. She could imitate many sounds.

"How do you do it Grandmother?"

"I practice changing the way I hold my mouth, how I make my throat tight or loose, everything until I find the right sound."

Many Smiles began to notice all the things he could do with his own voice. He could speak high and quickly like a mouse. After a while, he would feel like a mouse. If he spoke high and slowly, he'd sound more like how he imagined a caterpillar would sound. He could speak high and have a breathy sound and then, he'd be speaking like a moth. He could make his voice screech and then he'd sound like a bat. He could speak high and have a cry in his voice and he'd make the voice of a dog. He could honk, like a goose or a young man of his age whose voice was growing low. In fact, young men and geese had the same voices.

3.7 *What Fire Taught Us:*
Using Music, Dance, and Fire
to Respond to the Story

"Grandfather, sometimes when you tell a story, you blow something onto the fire that causes a huge fireball. How is this done?" Seagull asked.

Grandfather laughed. "I learned by experimenting with fire to identify different ways many things burn. Some burn in different colors, some burn quicker, some burn slower. I remember once in my youth we traveled south for many days and I saw the catalpa tree. The fire made from its dried branches squeaks and cracks more than any stick I had ever come across. The burning wood actually moves like a snake within the fire. Let me tell you a story.

"Once, long ago, Our People had a Chief who loved to hear stories. However, as time went on, he found that his hearing, which was very sharp, had become dull.

"Well, this Chief was well-respected because he had a talent for making himself understood without words. This was useful because when people from other tribes came who could not speak the language of The People, he was able to communicate.

"One day, he issued an invitation to seven Storytellers, each from one of the different districts. He would hold a celebration, where stories would be told, but no words could be used. Stories could be told through dance, through fire, or through music. Of course, being unable to hear, everyone wondered how he would hear the musicians." Pausing, Little Hawk touched his heart.

"In a neighboring village lived a Chief who loved stories as well. As time went on, he found that his sight, which had been as sharp as an eagle's, had become limited.

"The blind Chief and the deaf Chief decided they would listen to the stories together." Little Hawk locked his fingers to show unity.

"The Storytellers would all tell the same story, the story of Mother Bear. Of course, you know that there are several versions of this story, so it was decided that it should be told in the following way…"

Mother Bear

(A traditional Mi'kmaw tale.)

In the fall of the year of the great famine, the families could not live in villages. The fish and plants were gone and everyone was sent to scout for food far and wide, so they could meet that spring and bring back enough dried stores for The People to eat and, perhaps by spreading out, everyone could find a place that the famine had not touched.

One small family, a father and his young son, headed into the Great Forest to hunt for anything to eat. The boy's mother had been called to the Ancestors the same day the boy had been born, five years before. The father was determined that his son was going to survive. He found tree bark, and mushrooms, and some small game. These they ate, but the child craved meat, and none could be found.

One day, the father discovered bear prints. He determined to trap the bear. This way, his son would have enough food to survive the winter.

The father and son found a cave with only one way in, and devised a clever trap. Any bear who entered the cave would be trapped inside. Through an opening at the top of the cave, the father would be able to take the bear with a lance.

From the very beginning, the father regretted that he was going to have to be treacherous in order to catch the bear, but what could he do? He had to feed his young son and winter was approaching. So he set and baited the trap with the last of his food. Together, the father and son returned to their wigwam and waited.

The next morning, they returned to the cave. The stone had fallen, and from the hole in the rocks above the cave, the father could see that he had captured a large, female, black bear.

Outside the cave, two bear cubs sat, crying for their mother. The father looked at his son. They would surely starve if they didn't eat this bear. How could he leave these two cubs without a mother? He loved his son, but he would not leave children orphaned. He and his son would find a way to survive. Using a log, he rolled the stone away from the cave, and let the bear escape.

The mother bear, whose name was Thunder Bear, walked up to the man and sniffed him. Then, she let out a mighty roar right in his face. He could feel her hot breath on his skin. He did not speak bear, so he did not understand that she had said, "Thank you for not leaving my children orphaned."

The winter was hard and the father did what he could to keep his son alive. Often, he only had enough food for one. He grew ill and weak. One night, the spirit of his wife came to him and told him it was time for him to come with her to the Fires of the Ancestors.

When the boy awoke the next morning, the snow lay thick on the ground, and his father would not awaken. The boy wandered and wept, but in the forest, the animals did not heed him.

All except one. In her den, Thunder Bear heard the boy weeping. She took pity on him and brought him into her home and decided to raise the boy as her own. She protected him from the cold with her heavy fur coat, and on warmer winter days, the boy played with his brothers, the two bear cubs.

The boy soon learned the language of the bear, and learned to play bear games. He learned how to sleep the long sleep of the winter, and in the springtime Thunder Bear taught the boy how to fish by tossing fish onto land.

In the springtime, the famine had ended and everyone once again lived together in the village. One day, a group of fishermen came to the edge of the water. To their amazement, they saw a mother bear and her three cubs; one of them wore no fur at all, just a head of hair! This bear was human!

Thunder Bear was big and could provide many meals, so the hunters resolved to take her, but the bear-boy spoke up. "My father starved before taking this mother and leaving her cubs orphaned. You have plenty of fish, brothers, please spare my mother, Thunder Bear."

From that day onward, we have never hunted a mother bear who has cubs.

And in the winter, in the cleverly hidden wigwams of the mother bears, the smoke rises from their smoke holes. When you see this smoke, you know that a mother bear is inside, sleeping with her cubs. She sleeps well because she knows Our People will not hunt a mother bear and leave her cubs orphaned.

"Now how would you tell that story with fire and wind?" Grandfather Little Hawk asked. "That was the first challenge. But the challenge really was teaching the fire how to do a proper call and response. For instance, I tell the story, and the fire, in its language, repeats what I say.

"At the celebration, many people tried to tell the story with fire. One built fires that represented the bears, one created a fireball when the bear roared, and even caused the logs to collapse when the bear's trap was sprung, but the Chiefs were not pleased.

"'The fire is not used in an effective way,' the deaf Chief complained. 'If a Storyteller were to tell me the story in this way, without expression or feeling, the story wouldn't work.'

"Other Storytellers used cattail seeds to make snow. The seed heads scattered into a blizzard. The deaf Chief shook his head. 'It looks like snow,' he said, 'but I don't *hear* the snow falling.'

"Then, another Storyteller, a young woman, took her turn in the fire circle. She built a very small fire, and struggled to keep it lit. She scratched around on the ground for coals and pieces of grass. The fire was dim, and everyone watching worried that she wouldn't even be able to keep the fire lit. In the story, when the bear was trapped, she took out a large, arm-length branch of kindling and laid it aside. She didn't add it to the fire. She produced some long, dry branches from her small pile of firewood. Acting the part of the bear, She pounded the ground with the sticks until they broke, and then stirred up the dust to symbolize the bear's roar. Everyone else had used a fireball of toasted flour blown onto the fire.

"When the snow fell, she blew four tufts of goose feather down into the air and watched them float. Some people actually discovered that the goose feather down made them shiver as they watched the individual tufts dance on the air currents.

"During the part of the story where the father went to tend the Fires of the Ancestors with his wife, the Storyteller placed a coal from the fire on a few oak leaves and blew a fireball. She arranged the branches she'd broken earlier into a separate pile. Then she extinguished the fire. The wigwam was in darkness. All anyone could see, if he strained, was one sad, orange coal gleaming like an eye in the darkness. The Storyteller added more leaves until the coal was hidden. The smell of smoke rose in the wigwam. All of a sudden, the leaves burst into flames, and the Storyteller placed the burning leaves into the pile of sticks she had created. The fire leaped through her fire structure, giving off both heat and light. The Storyteller created a small, steady fire. Then she produced an armful of kindling which she broke. It snapped easily. She stacked it by the fire so that everyone could see it, but she didn't burn it. Finally, she lit some dried tobacco bundles and blew on them. These she passed to the people and indicated that they should blow on the bundle and pass it on. The deaf Chief was very pleased.

"'You understand!' he proclaimed. 'Your fire responded to the feeling of the story and it also taught a lesson. You spared the wood at the end so it could kindle other fires and at the end, you shared the bounty of the fire with the people. In my heart, I *heard* your story.'"

"This is a good story, Grandfather. I have learned not only that the fire should respond to the story and not attempt to tell the story, but also that fine-powdered pollen and flour browned on a hot rock and blown on the fire will create a fireball."

"Yes, Seagull. And goose feather down and fluffy plant seeds can be used to create the feeling of snow."

Grandmother laughed. "It's best to learn by trying different woods and plants in your own fire. But fire is not the only effect in good storytelling. You can use the sounds outside the wigwam and even collect plants for special effects."

Dancing Rain rose and walked to the part of the wigwam where storytelling bags were stored. She reached into one of the bags, pulled out a few strands of goose feather down, and blew them into the air like snowflakes. Grandfather started to speak.

"During the cold winter, the snow fell without stopping."

Next, she took a branch of cedar and dipped it in a bowl of water. "The rains fell." Grandmother waved the cedar branch. Seagull and Many Smiles felt droplets of water.

"You can use pinches of fat and grease and leeks in the fire to make your listeners smell food and, of course, you can use herbs for smudges.

"But remember, my Grandchildren, what the story teaches. Music, fire, and dance are responses to the *emotion* of the story. It is the *feeling* you want to express with the music, not the actual sounds. When the bear is caught, and the cubs are distressed, show the feeling of these sounds in the beating of the drums and the feeling you would have if you heard the high cry of the cub's voice and the moaning of the mother," Dancing Rain explained.

"In the celebration, the successful musicians used a conch shell for the call of the bear. Even though it did not sound like a roar, it *felt* like one. It startled the people and was loud and immediate. The cold and the snow was a low flute playing with much breath in its voice, and the spirit was a moose call, deep within a birchbark tube.

"Of course, it's even better when you invent sounds for the story. The storytelling musicians did just that. One of the musicians played a drum and the other blew on a leaf blade to create a sad, desperate cry when the boy was alone. Then with rattles and drums, the musicians let the people help make the sounds of the bear's home, all full of life and fun and sound. And to create the feel of the sound of fish, well, my grandfather once taught me the secret of playing river rocks like instruments."

Dancing Rain handed Little Hawk two smooth river rocks. Little Hawk turned them over in his hands, pretending to be confused. "Grandfather, you're telling me that I can make music from two river rocks?" he spoke with the voice of a child.

"'This is true, Grandson.'

"My grandfather held out his left hand, his fingers pressed tightly together to make a cup so the fingertips and the thumb and the palm could hold water. Onto the fingertips on the side of the thumb he placed one river rock. And then with another rock he tapped."

Little Hawk demonstrated his grandfather's actions.

"But, Grandfather, how is this music?"

Little Hawk's eyes jumped from Many Smiles, to Seagull, to Dancing Rain and he smiled as if they knew his secret.

"Listen." Little Hawk tapped on the river rock, opening his fingers one by one like petals of the flower and closing them again. As he tapped, the pitch the rock made changed from low to high to low again.

"It's amazing!" Seagull smiled.

"Just as every rock holds all the stories, in every footprint is a musical instrument, in every leaf a rattle or a whistle waits for you to awaken it.

"I could teach you," Little Hawk said, "how to make a blade of grass scream like a gull, or a leaf sing. Instead, I will simply tell you that if you blow across the thin edge of a leaf or a blade of grass, it will make a sound. The tighter you pull leaf or the blade of grass, the higher the sound will get.

"I will tell you that by clapping your hands, or moving your fingers along your throat, you can produce interesting sounds. And then I will tell you to play. Go out and make it rain and snow, make the grass sing, make the conch shell bellow, make the acorn cap whistle. Make rattles out of everything: deer toes, sticks, shells.

"Some of the musicians at the celebration were honored by the blind Chief and the deaf Chief. The other musicians agreed that these musicians had techniques that they were all anxious to learn.

"'How could you tell they were playing so well?' the blind Chief asked the deaf Chief. They both spoke by voice and sign.

"'I watched the faces of the people. I could tell by their response to the music exactly what part of the story the musicians were telling.'

"Our grandfather was one of those musicians," Dancing Rain commented.

"The same one that was a great fish hunter?" Many Smiles asked.

"No. Our other grandfather, my mother's father, Singing Whale. He told me how the Chief was moved by their performance and invited them to dine with him that evening. Later, they watched the dancers. They, too, flowed with the call and response to the feeling of the story, not to the telling of it.

"And now, my children, it is your turn to tell a story. What smells can you create by throwing dried cedar on the hot coals, or tobacco, or onion grass? How can you fill the wigwam with light, movement, smells, and sounds? Now I will send you to go and play. Let us see what you can bring back."

Many Smiles and Seagull wondered what they could bring back. The early spring air was cold and none of the plants had sprouted yet.

"I will give you a little direction that may help. First, as you play, make sure nothing you put in your mouth is poisonous. You must know that by buzzing your lips into a tube you can make very interesting sounds. You must also know that blowing across an opening will make a sound. Learn from me.

"Spread your hands to make a moth, your fingers will be the wings and the joints of your thumb that have fingernails will be the antennae of the moth. Now look at the shape the two antennae make. Where your thumbs come together they form a sharp point, like the outline of a spear. You can put any kind of cup, like an acorn cap, so that it is held tightly against the place where the thumbs meet. If you can see the edge of the acorn cap just above where the antennae start, then you're holding the acorn cap correctly.

"You must hold the acorn cap very tightly so that all around it is pressed against the skin of your thumb, except for the top part showing above the moth antennae. Remember, press it tight to your fingers. Rest your bottom lip on the area where your two thumbs meet, and rest your top lip along the knuckles of the thumbs, and blow. Blow hard and soft, adjust your thumbs, change the angle, and you will make the acorn cap whistle.

"Call and respond to the flow of the story through fire, music, and movement. Practice these skills. In fact, I would like to see the two of you tell that same story of the bear in all three forms. Let the feeling of the story speak. And now I will tell you what happened at the end of the celebration.

"The Storytellers combined their skills. A Storyteller spoke the words of the story, and the musicians played, the dancers danced, and the firekeepers kept the fire. The people declared that it was wonderful."

Many Smiles and Seagull left the next morning to greet the sunrise, as they had been doing since Many Smiles had returned. They decided that instead of telling the story of the bear, they would tell the story of the first morning when they had welcomed the dawn, and how the seagulls had come to the high land to join them. Each morning they practiced, saying part of the story and then responding with the feeling they had felt. At first, Many Smiles was frustrated. "What is the sound of the Sun rising?"

"I think that is a question you can't answer, Many Smiles. I think you better ask, what is the music in your heart when you see the Sun rise?"

"It starts so quietly, Seagull, almost as if it's no sound at all, and then it builds until it is all around me."

"And the fire is the same. The rising of the Sun is like the smell of smoke before the fire. You can *smell* it coming. And the dance, you already know."

Many Smiles and Seagull built an unusual fire. It was made with twigs, brush, and small branches. It was dug into a trench that was partially covered with stones. It ran in a quarter circle around the outdoor fire pit, and then it traveled in a straight line from east to west, to the main fire pit. When Little Hawk and Dancing Rain came to watch, the Sun had just set. Many Smiles kept a small fire burning deep inside a pit in the ground. He began to beat the drum and Seagull danced, her hands reaching towards the Moon. As the breeze picked up, Seagull responded to it.

"My Grandfather and Grandmother once taught me how to speak to the wind and welcome the stars into the sky. Then, it was our task, mine and Many Smiles, to welcome the Sun as we would a dear relative. I greeted the dawn breezes and waited for the morning."

Many Smiles lit the fire. It glowed deep within the trench and started travelling toward the fire pit.

Many Smiles added his drumbeat to the song, the song of the awakening life after the long night. He felt a breeze come and he shook his rattle.

The fire sometimes glimmered, like an early ray of sunshine on the water. It crept toward the fire pit, towards its dawning. Many Smiles watched Seagull dance and, as she had done before, she pulled the dawn into the sky.

From where she was standing Seagull couldn't see that the fire was almost at the tinder that would make the main fire structure burst into flame. She had to finish the dance quickly. Many Smiles sang out a note that rose, like the Sun. Seagull understood. She bent to the Earth and pulled the Sun into the sky. The tinder lit, and the tower of kindling caught fire. Little Hawk and Dancing Rain were bathed in the warmth and light of the fire. Seagull held her body in the position of a hovering seagull. Many Smiles made the laughing sound of a seagull with a blade of grass.

"And my sisters, for whom I am named," Seagull declared, "danced the Sun into the sky with me. That's when Many Smiles decided that he must return to his own village. Right there, at sunrise, he knew what he must do. He went back so he could share the gifts of his first moose hunt with his people. From childhood, Many Smiles was taught that the one who shares and cares for others, to the best of his or her ability, is much respected by The People.

"We are young, but the spirit of our bodies, and the spirit of our souls are clear," Seagull said. "After three winters have passed, Many Smiles will return to his people for the Council. The Grand Chief of the Seven Districts will visit his grandfather's village. The council will meet to discuss some very important matters, and Becomes Unseen thought that it was important that Many Smiles be part of those decisions. But at dawn, we decided that when he returns from that council, we are going to ask my father and mother's permission to cut our hair, in the way of newlyweds, and to allow Many Smiles to become part of our family as my husband."

Dancing Rain and Little Hawk looked at each other. "My children!" Dancing Rain said. "This is indeed a remarkable story, one that I hope you both tell for many years to come. You are both still so very young! Many Smiles said he would spend many seasons as a man before he married." Dancing Rain looked at Seagull. "Why did he change his mind?"

Seagull grinned. "Grandparents, allow me to finish my story. I think it will explain everything."

And she held her arms like the wings of a hovering seagull. "The morning sky was still dark, but the seagulls were singing. Before the Sun had risen, my sisters, the seagulls knew. And in those hours before dawn, they perched and waited with us for the new day. Many Smiles tended the fire. I turned to him and said, 'They know, Many Smiles,' and he said, 'I also know, and you do, too. Our lives are joined. So even if our childhood isn't quite over yet, let's always watch the Sun rise together.'"

The seasons passed, and Many Smiles and Seagull practiced the many lessons they had learned from their elders. Many Smiles remained with Seagull through the next three winters and returned to his people in the spring to speak at the Council and await The Great Decision. The Clan Mothers had met and agreed that the decision was good. The women had met and had also agreed to the decision. And so it was, that after sixty-three councils, the time of the Great Decision was finally at hand.

Four

TELLING THE TRUTH: Lessons from Adulthood[3]

4.1 The Shortest Story: Focusing on What is Important

"After you marry, you will be leaving us."

Seagull hugged Little Hawk. "Yes, Grandfather, we will be going further north to join the new clan. It was discussed and agreed to. We will be at least one day's walk from your people, and two days' walk from Many Smiles' grandfather."

"The tribes have spoken, the councils have met. This discussion began before you and Many Smiles were born, when our village separated from your grandfather's village. Each generation, Our People have prospered and grown numerous, and so for sixty-three years, we have discussed creating this new village. Now all that remains is to choose the chief. Many Smiles' uncle, Becomes Unseen, and our tribesmen, One Moccasin, are both being considered for the position of Chief."

---

3   Refer to curriculum p.200–201

Many Smiles approached, carrying a basket full of fish. "The Great Water has been generous today. I heard you talking. I hope I'm not interrupting."

"No, Grandson. This concerns you. The two Clan Mothers have met. Becomes Unseen will guide the first winter camp and One Moccasin will guide the first summer camp. This way, both leaders can learn what it would mean to be chief of the new village, and then together we can decide who will lead the new village."

"Becomes Unseen is a great hunter. North of here, we may have to range to hunt the caribou. Who can move better than Becomes Unseen? I do not doubt One Moccasin's skills, but a summer camp is easier to run than a winter camp. I hope everyone considers that."

"Grandson Many Smiles, you will have your chance to speak of these things to the Council, but you know that both your uncle and One Moccasin are wise and they will do what is best for The People, otherwise, the Clan Mothers would not have selected these two in the first place. One Moccasin does not have a Storyteller in his family circle and, if your uncle is chosen, he will want you both as his Storytellers. This is why no matter who becomes chief, you will be asked to go north and be the Storytellers of the new village.

"Two nights from today, the men of both tribes are gathering at Second Water, half-a-day's journey for both clans. We will hold a friendly gathering, and you will tell a story. It will be the story of what you have learned about being a Storyteller."

"But Grandfather, you have taught me so much, the story will last forever!"

Grandfather smiled, shook his head, and lifted the fingers of his right hand. "Grandson, you will use no more words than I can count on one hand."

"But Grandfather, what you ask is impossible! And Seagull will not be there to caretake the fire if it's to be a gathering of men."

"You have two days to prepare. Go to the wigwam, Grandson." He looked at Seagull. "Talk together. Ask the wind and the trees and mostly Grandmother Rock for help. Many Smiles will tell a good story. Sometimes the best stories are the shortest."

Many Smiles and Seagull returned to the wigwam. Seagull had been busy learning how to build a wigwam. She had just rebuilt a wigwam for Basking Turtle because that spring, Basking Turtle's wife had made the journey to the Land of the Ancestors.

Many Smiles paced and muttered to himself, and twisted his storytelling necklace. "We're having a gathering of the men. Becomes Unseen and One Moccasin must decide which of them should be chief of the new village. And at the beginning of this gathering, I'm supposed to tell a story and use only five words. And it must be the story of all that I have learned from Grandfather Little Hawk and Grandmother Dancing Rain. I don't know what I am going to do."

"One Moccasin is your friend," said Seagull. "He is a good man. Remember how he welcomed you to our tribe with a game of Waltes? He remained unmarried for a long time because he thought I was going to be his wife, even though I was much younger than him. Still, he congratulated you when we announced that we were going to be married. He is a good and fair man. Becomes Unseen is your uncle. Many times you've told me how he taught you how to hunt. He is a good and fair man. Either way, Our People will have a good leader and you will tell a good story."

"I thank you for your confidence in me. Tomorrow morning, let's go to the Eastern Sun and see what it has to say."

The next morning, Many Smiles and Seagull called and responded to the wind. The wind came, they welcomed it, and then the breeze passed on.

Where are you going, Wind? Many Smiles wondered. Will you travel the whole Earth and return here? Or maybe you are the grandson of the wind that made my great-grandfather's hair dance when he was a child.

After they had called and responded to the wind, they played with their pouches and pebbles. Seagull reminded Many Smiles that their pebbles were the great-grandchildren of the great-grandchildren of Grandmother Rock. They ate some dried moose meat, boiled into a stew with cattail shoots, sweetened with sorrel and dried plum fruit. They also had ash cakes with maple syrup.

"Wife-to-Be, we are Storytellers, and we are the great-grandchildren of the grandchildren of the children of First Child, who wore in his pouch the child of Grandmother Rock. If Grandfather wants me to tell in five words what I have learned from him, how can I do that when the story has taken so many generations to come to me?"

"Husband-to-Be, I am a child of the Two-Legged Nation. This is what I know: Our ways are what we pass to our children. We don't teach our children to breathe through their gills. We don't teach our daughters to lay eggs. What we pass along is the walking, the fire, the love, and the stories of Our People.

"Grandfather Little Hawk knows you are a human. He knows you are capable of telling this story. I do, too. I will help you prepare. The same night the men are at Council, the women will come to our camp and hold their own gathering. I will tell the same story to the women and children that you tell to the men. Your story is about how life itself made you a Storyteller. Do not think you can own this story or can create it. The story created *you*."

The evening of the Council arrived.

The tiny six-legged ants watched the Two-Leggeds come.

"Oh, no, we are going to be visited by the Two-Legged giants," said the warrior ant.

The Clan Mother of the ants calmed the warrior by stroking his head with her feelers. "Don't worry, young warrior. The Two-Leggeds bring much destruction it is true, and after they come, we have much work to do. But they always bring food. If they are meeting and building a tiny forest fire the way they usually do, it means that we will be able to live off what they leave for a very long time."

Many Smiles gently brushed an ant off his leg. The special smell of the woods in the dry season filled the Storyteller with memories of playing with his cousins on long summer days.

"Oh, men, I was resting so nicely in this tree," the Red Hawk complained. "Did you really have to meet right here, under my tree?"

Rain had not fallen in many days. The streams were low, barely trickling. Many Smiles heard a Red Hawk cry and fly deeper into the woods.

"Look, father," said the young birchbark tree. "Here are our friends, the Two-Leggeds. They bring us many gifts and they honor our ancestors by living inside their skins."

"It is true, my son, they take very good care of us. Why, just the other day when Brother Elm's branch dried and the branch was rubbing against my bark, up climbs a young Two-Legged, dressed in deerskin, moving like a squirrel, with clever raccoon-like hands. I know that I'm grateful for the Two-Legged who took the dried branch that was rubbing against me. He helped me to heal that thin part of my bark."

"Look father," said the young birchbark tree, "This must be a Two-Legged medicine ceremony just for us! They are removing all the dead branches from the trees, and they are stacking them in a pile. It feels good to be rid of my dried-up branches. And look, they are honoring Great-Grandfather Birch who now grows his leaves in the forest of the ancestors. Listen to their songs of thanks! Look how carefully they remove the bark from where he has fallen. I think Great-Grandfather will honor these Two-Leggeds by releasing fire from his wood."

After the men had gathered firewood, they sat in an area shaded by birch trees. They would sleep there that night on the mossy ground. The light wind embraced the leaves, dancing across the stream from the southwest. The wind was in no hurry. The trees, the southwest wind, and the ants seemed to say, "Welcome Two-Leggeds, this is a good place to be." The Red Hawk disagreed.

Many Smiles leaned against the cool body of a grandfather elm. His own grandfather, Deer Cloud, as well as Little Hawk and Becomes Unseen, leaned against the same great tree. In this place of peace, Many Smiles knew that all he had to do was respond to the call of the land, and his story would be a success. In a buckskin bag, several objects waited to reveal themselves and help tell the story.

The day was still hot, and the setting Sun was still powerful, so the men decided to cool off in the stream before starting the fire.

The stream knew Many Smiles. It had conversed with him many times, and the stream had shared its wisdom with this curious young man. Many Smiles had arrived before the others, and had greeted his old friend, the stream. In the manner of all streams, the water greeted Many Smiles by cooling his feet against smooth rocks.

"Stream, old friend, this night I have no Caretaker. My wife-to-be is not with me. I have crossed you many times, I have played in your currents, and walked on your surface in the winter. You have provided me with fish and turtles. Right now, you cool my hot body. Now I ask you to be my Caretaker for this important story I am about to tell."

The stream answered in its own language, offering its sweet water, whispering over the shallows, twirling around boulders. "Yes," it said, "I will be your Caretaker."

Many Smiles knew that the most comfortable seats would be reserved for the elders and that the young ones would sit furthest from the fire. Before anyone arrived, he arranged the clearing so the most comfortable spots to sit were on the eastern edge of the clearing, furthest from the stream. He cleared an area for the fire pit so that the people would choose to sit just the way he needed for the story to be told correctly.

The Sun had set. Great-Grandfather Birch had offered the fire from its wood. The men had eaten the food and had scattered enough to keep the ants happy for many moons. The breeze and the fire played together like two young puppies, wrestling and tumbling. Even the grumpy Red Hawk sleepily returned to his perch to watch the gathering.

Many Smiles had arranged things perfectly. The men sat in a row with the elders furthest from the stream to the East, and the youngest sitting next to the stream to the West.

The Chiefs stood. Two Wolves, the Chief of the clan of Becomes Unseen, spoke. He had a wide face and eyes that were intense like an eagle's. His skin was tough and furrowed like tree bark. He stood straight and stern, his body was a spear. He spoke very quietly, loudly enough to be heard, but not so loud that he would disturb the other creatures in the forest.

"After today, we will be three villages. A chief must be chosen for the new village. The Clan Mothers have made a decision. We have come to discuss preparations for the celebration and for the new village. We think it is good to begin the gathering with a story. We have asked Little Hawk to tell us a story."

Little Hawk? But I was going to tell the story. I was prepared, Many Smiles frowned.

Little Hawk stood. Many Smiles noticed that while the Chief had a rigid, spear-like body, Little Hawk's body seemed fluid, like the river, like a breeze, like the smoke. "I see that we have young men and elders here." Little Hawk moved as he spoke. His voice carried into the night. "I see that we have people who were children long ago when we were all part of one clan, and I see those who have lived among both our clans."

Did I hear wrong? Many Smiles wondered. *Didn't Little Hawk ask me to tell this story?*

"My brothers, much is unresolved about this new clan. Who will be chief? Who will be Puoin? Who will be Keeper of the Flame? Who will be Clan Mother? This we do not know. What we do know is that Many Smiles and Seagull, his wife-to-be, will be the Storytellers of the new village no matter who becomes chief. I have asked Many Smiles to tell us the story of how he came to be a Storyteller. I have asked him to tell us the story using no more than five words."

The men grew silent. Little Hawk stepped back, so that his face seemed to glow in the light of the fire, while his body was in darkness. It seemed he was floating in the air. Many Smiles walked around the fire. He positioned himself behind a tree, just behind the people. In one hand, he held a drum. In the other, he held the items he had collected for this storytelling.

Little Hawk went back to sit among the elders. Many Smiles waited in silence, counting his own heartbeats pounding in his ears. He calmed his breath and the stream, his Caretaker, called to him and he felt reassured.

Dramatically, with one loud, unexpected beat of the drum, he leapt from behind the tree, leaving the drum behind. No one expected him to emerge where he did. The men were startled. Many Smiles appeared and danced from the elders to the young men sitting by the stream. He held a rolled up hide in front of him. The elders laughed. The cousins laughed. All of those who remembered that Many Smiles had once been named Startle Drumming understood the meaning of his entrance.

With a flourish, Many Smiles unrolled the hide. A handful of items fell to the ground. Silhouetted by the fire, he grabbed one of the items and raised it in the air so that all could see that this was a small version of a spear. Now, Many Smiles moved like a small boy, like Startle Drumming. He took the spear and presented it to Two Wolves. "Pass it on, our teacher."

He led Two Wolves to the spot where Becomes Unseen was standing. Two Wolves had taught Becomes Unseen to hunt. "Pass it on, our teacher."

Many Smiles reached out his hands and took the spear. Becomes Unseen had taught Many Smiles to hunt. Many Smiles danced from east to west, from oldest to youngest, and touched each gently with the handle of the spear. "Pass it on, our teacher."

Finally, he presented the small spear to the youngest man, Sea Mink. This was a very special gathering for Sea Mink. He was given special permission to attend because his clan had agreed that he would be the first young man to take a moose in the autumn. Sea Mink sat closest to the stream. Many Smiles handed the spear to Sea Mink. "Pass it on, our teacher," and pointed to his Caretaker, the stream. The young man looked questioningly at Many Smiles. The Storyteller guided Sea Mink's hands until he held the spear over the stream, and repeated, "Pass it on, our teacher."

The boy dropped the wooden spear in the stream and the stream carried the spear away. The spear drifted out of sight, until it got caught between a pair of boulders, as Many Smiles had intended.

Many Smiles danced back to where his items were scattered around the fire. In his hands, he raised a damaged wooden bowl that could not be repaired, but was perfect for the story. His fingers hid the cracks in the bowl. He pretended to play the game of Waltes. He offered the bowl to One Moccasin's grandfather, the oldest man at the gathering and the husband of the Clan Mother. "Pass it on, our teacher." One Moccasin's father passed the bowl to One Moccasin, who passed the bowl to Many Smiles, whom he had taught to play the game.

Then Many Smiles passed the bowl from oldest to youngest. In the end, the youngest, Sea Mink, passed the bowl into the stream, and the bowl floated out of sight, until it was caught, like the spear, between the two boulders.

Many Smiles motioned with his hands that everyone should stand. Then he danced over to the tree where he had put his drum. A small toy replica of his real drum, made of a worn-out birchbark basket, lay on the ground in front of the fire. This he passed to Little Hawk. "Pass it on, our teacher," Many Smiles sang, and Little Hawk passed the birchbark drum as Many Smiles kept the heartbeat on his real drum. "Pass it on," the people sang.

When the toy drum reached Sea Mink, it was given to the stream. Many

Smiles stopped drumming and danced to the spot in front of his grandfather. Every man was still on his feet. Many Smiles hugged his grandfather with all the love he could possibly feel for someone whose story had *told him*. "Pass it on, our teacher," Many Smiles said. Elders hugged grandsons, and the circle closed. Many Smiles walked down to the river and thanked it for caretaking his story. He retrieved the small spear, the broken bowl, and the toy drum from between the rocks in the stream and put them back into his bag.

As he walked back to the gathering, Many Smiles felt happy. The story was complete. Tonight's story was not a story that Many Smiles had told. It was the story that had told *him*. In fact, this is the story that has told all of creation into being since the beginning: *Pass it on.*

4.2 The Great Preparation: Filling the Space, Part One

The Moon of Berry Ripening was a time of great preparation. Uncle Becomes Unseen was gathering squares of birchbark with Seagull and Many Smiles.

"Whatever you find useful, put it in your gathering basket. We will have plenty of time to sort once we arrive at the Winter Camp."

"How many people will be in our camp, Uncle?" Many Smiles asked. The taller man smiled at Many Smiles. The young man had grown strong and slender, and since he had been married to Seagull, he wore his hair short. He was a hard worker and a good hunter. The group needed a Storyteller. What the council had asked him to do would be very difficult.

"I know it is not our way to maintain a village during the cold moons," One Moccasin's father, Chief Silver Eagle had said. "We do not know you, Becomes Unseen, but your Chief says that you are a fine hunter and you have shared much meat with your people. We need to know if you can do a remarkable thing and keep your people together through the winter. Such was the challenge of my great-great-grandfather when he established your village. And such will be your challenge."

Many Smiles waited for the others to speak and then it was his turn. "Our Chief Silver Eagle has said that Becomes Unseen is challenged to keep these people together during the Winter Camp. The council has set the number of people at fifty-three, including some grandparents and some children. They say that this is the way our village was established long ago. My uncle is a good hunter and a wise man. My wife and I will go with him and live in his Winter Camp. I encourage my uncle to accept this challenge because I believe he would serve The People well as chief."

One Moccasin was the next to speak. "Many Smiles is a wise Storyteller. He reminded us with his story yesterday that this is not a contest between men. The most important thing we can do is pass the lessons of the grandparents along in a good way. I have been asked to gather one hundred and fifty people in a new, warm-weather village at the side of the Great Water. What you ask of Becomes Unseen is an even greater task. Becomes Unseen, if you accept and accomplish your task, you will have proven yourself. I will do whatever I can to help you through the winter."

Becomes Unseen spoke. "One Moccasin is a good leader, a good man. I say that I understand the wisdom of the Long-Ago Grandfathers, and I honor them. As the chief, I must pass on their wisdom to my Great-Great-Grandchildren. Winter Camp is often a time of danger and hunger. This winter will be the first time in many years that this area will be hunted. We will bring a good supply of food with us.

"One Moccasin, you are brave and wise. I would be honored to have you as part of our winter village. The Council has agreed that one of us should be chief. If, in the Moon of Berry Ripening one summer from now, the council decides to name you Chief, I will help your village prepare for winter and ask my Chief to grant a large portion of what we gather for the new village."

Becomes Unseen had met with the fifty-three, and spoke to the women as well as the men. He even asked the children what they thought. Now, the whole camp was working hard, and One Moccasin was leading the effort of his people to contribute a generous amount of food and materials.

In the wigwam of Little Hawk, Grandmother Dancing Rain told a story to Seagull and Many Smiles. "Remember my granddaughter, that the Storyteller and the Caretaker must fill the whole wigwam with the story. This is a great time to share what you have learned with The People of both villages. But tonight, Little Hawk and I will tell the stories. You two have something important to do tomorrow."

The next day, while both clans were still in the village, Many Smiles and Seagull had their own celebration: A wedding.

4.3 Seagull Breaks Her Leg:
Filling the Space, Part Two

Later that week, as preparations continued for the new clan, Many Smiles and Seagull had a chance to talk about the storytelling they had witnessed.

"Someday we will be able to fill the whole space with story the way that Grandmother and Grandfather did," Seagull said.

"I have watched your Grandfather Little Hawk and Grandmother Dancing Rain tell stories since I was very little. I have never stopped feeling like an excited child when I listen to them," Many Smiles replied.

Little Hawk appeared at the opening of the new wigwam Seagull had built. "May I enter?"

Seagull greeted her relative. "Please sit high in our wigwam, Grandfather Little Hawk. We were just talking about this week's story. Everyone was so excited after the story was over. Everyone felt that you were telling the story to them, no matter where they sat in the crowd."

"Grandchildren, let us go outside."

The day was sunny and hot. "I think I'm going to go and sit in the shade." The young couple followed Grandfather Little Hawk as he walked down a trail and finally found the tree he was looking for. The tree was no longer green. The sea breezes had shrugged off its branches and now the bark of the tree was a home to many insects. The tree resembled a wigwam pole. This pole cast a long, thin shadow on the ground. Little Hawk sat in the thin shadow and invited Seagull and Many Smiles to sit in its shade. He sat quietly for a while. The Sun shifted, doing its usual circle dance in the sky. Soon, Many Smiles and Seagull had to move to stay in the shade.

"When I ran barefoot in the summers of my boyhood, I once heard a story from a respected hunter of our tribe. The story was about a hunt, where a Bobcat had disrupted the flow of the hunt. It was a wonderful story, but the hunter who told it was no Storyteller. We felt we were listening to a conversation that we had not been invited to hear. The hunter sat before us and stared into the fire. He told his story. He never moved his arms, never looked at our faces, never stood to show us things.

"Dancing Rain and I knew that we wanted to be Storytellers. We noticed the way people were listening. They were respectful of the hunter, yet I noticed that those on the edges of the gathering were looking toward the horizon and were playing with pebbles. We were sitting toward the back of the gathering, almost directly in front of the Storyteller. We were very aware of every stray noise. The story cast a faint shadow so that those who paid the most attention were those directly in front of the Storyteller. The hunter's storytelling was like the shade of this tree.

"The Storyteller who focuses on his story casts a thin shadow. Outside of that shadow, those who listen may feel uncomfortable. You can see this tree from far away, even if you do not sit in its shadow, but the tree no longer reaches out with leafy branches, so its shadow does not touch you, it does not give you comfort."

Little Hawk rose to his feet. "Grandchildren, let us sit by a different tree." They walked until they reached a growth of young maples. One tree had thick branches that bore many children and grandchildren and great-grandchildren branches. Each of these was covered by leaves. The tree was not tall, but it cast a vast shadow on the ground. In the shade, cool ferns grew. "Grandchildren, do you realize that this tree is not as tall as the one we were sitting under before?"

"Yes, Grandfather," Many Smiles and Seagull answered in unison.

"And whose shade do you prefer?"

"This young maple," they both answered.

Little Hawk smiled. "My grandmother once told a story about a time when she was a girl and found a caterpillar. She picked up the caterpillar, and brought it to a tree near her wigwam. She told the story so well, and she made us all feel such a part of the story, that I believed I could see the caterpillar. She looked right at me and she knew that I *believed*. Dancing

Rain was sitting with our mother. They were on the other side of the gathering. Yet, Dancing Rain felt that my grandmother was looking directly at *her*. Not just those at the center, but *all of us* sat in the shadow of her story.

"By the fire, sat her sister, who was her Caretaker. And because I watched with the eyes of the Storyteller, I noticed that the Caretaker would move to the edge of the gathering and watch the people. If she saw that a small child fell outside that shadow of the story, she somehow signaled my grandmother. My grandmother would move close to that child, and bring the child back into the shadow of the story.

"The hunter's story was very dramatic, yet when he told it, I soon lost interest. The story of the caterpillar was simple, but we children spoke about it for months afterwards. I asked Grandmother how she had made the story of the caterpillar so interesting, and how was it that my mind had wandered during the story of the bobcat.

"'When you are alone and nobody's watching, do you sometimes act like a little child, and dance, and spin around, and do somersaults?' my grandmother asked me.

"'Why don't you do these things when other people are around?'

"'If I acted that way, everyone would laugh at me.'

"My grandmother smiled. 'It's just so,' she said. Then she put her hand on my shoulder. 'You are afraid that people will laugh at you or you're afraid your parents will not like the way that you behave. But when you're alone, only the trees and the birds can watch, and the little voice inside of you that tells you how to act says, *Now it's your time to be free. Have no fear.* Well, the hunter who told the story must be a brave hunter. He was not at all concerned about the bobcat. I do not know if I would have had the same courage to face the bobcat that he did. But when he told the story, he did not feel the energy and the expectation of the people. Instead, he feared what they would say about him.'

"Then, my grandmother hugged me. 'Do something silly,' she said. She sat on the ground and waited. She stared at me. I waved my hands and said, 'Yoi Yii Yau!' But I held my energy back. I don't know why.

"Then my grandmother jumped to her feet. She put her face close to mine and cocked her head like a dog. Then she barked at me. I thought it was the funniest thing I ever heard. I did not know what to do.

"'You are my puppy!' she yelped. She sniffed my shoulder, so I sniffed hers. Soon, I was crawling around like a dog, yelping and barking.

"'Grandson, do you see? I did not hesitate to be silly. You needed me to invite you not to be afraid. The Storyteller can never worry if the listeners like the story. The Storyteller must give the people permission to respond. At first, the people will be hesitant. But somewhere in the crowd, there is always a brave listener. This may be the person who enters the circle, talking, laughing, attracting others to respond. Call to that person and invite a response. A brave listener will lead the others.'"

Little Hawk smiled at Many Smiles. "My grandmother taught me an important lesson about storytelling. Before we tell a story, if I am the Caretaker, I notice who reflects the most energy, who would make very good Storytellers. When I choose the people to participate in my stories, I make sure to choose one of those who wish to be part of the story. I also notice which people are shyest. And into the hands of these shy people, I put rattles. Do you understand why?"

Many Smiles pondered the question. "Grandfather, I think I do. You know that your listeners, the ones who are brave, will sing and dance and speak during the storytelling. You know that the shy will be quiet. So you give them a rattle."

"I sometimes whisper encouraging words or smile to show I approve of the way they shake the rattle."

"Grandfather," Seagull took a bowl of stew and handed it to Little Hawk. "Sometimes you have two hundred listeners. How can you make your shadow so big that everyone can sit beneath it?"

"I move among the people so that they can sense my good feelings for them. I remember that their ancestors are now with my ancestors and we are all related. My Caretaker also helps me watch and remember. Every story can be a way of filling a space with love. Tomorrow, at the evening fire you, Seagull, will tell a story. Remember that these are your people and you love them. Fill the space with the shadow of your story. Let it spread over each person there, and the people's understanding will be lifted, and they will respond with love. Many Smiles will help you as the Caretaker for your story."

Sometimes The Invisible Ones act in unexpected ways. That is how it was that afternoon. Seagull was helping to carry a basket of fish to the village, when she stepped between two large rocks and fell. Her foot was wedged between the rocks when she fell, and badly injured her leg bone. Two strong women carried her and the basket of fish back to the village. Seagull's father, the Puoin, pulled the bone back into place. He took some finely pounded moss and mixed it with powdered fir tree sap. He wrapped the leg in birchbark, and tied seven splints around the birchbark. Seagull was not permitted to walk for half a moon.

"How will I be able to tell the story now?" she asked. "Maybe you should tell the story tonight, Many Smiles." Many Smiles visited the wigwam of Little Hawk and Dancing Rain.

"This is a great challenge," Dancing Rain said. "It is possible for Seagull to fill the whole space, and to cast a wide shadow even if she cannot move. I have seen it done. Remember, a tree may be rooted, but it can still cast a wide shadow."

"But how?" Many Smiles asked.

"As with all shade trees, each twig has its leaf."

"You're telling us that we have to figure this out for ourselves aren't you?"

"I cannot tell you what to do. If you were a dog, I would say bark and howl. If you were a bird, I would say sing. You are Many Smiles and Seagull. So fill the space like Many Smiles and Seagull. Play. Call and respond. Love."

Many Smiles hurried back to his wife.

"What did Grandmother say?"

"We can do this, my wife. I will be your Caretaker, and you will tell the story. And you will fill the space. We will find a way for you to walk through play, call and response, and love."

"If we can perform such a wondrous thing through play, call and response, and love, then why just walk? Why not fly as well?"

The rest of the day, and into the next they worked on a wonderful story.

The next night, the elders sat in a wide semicircle around the fire. Close to the fire, perched on a chair made of driftwood, sat Seagull. Many Smiles paid careful attention to all the people who entered the circle. He noticed among the adults and among the children, who were the most talkative and who were the most likely Storytellers at the edge of the assembly. One girl in particular laughed and poked her brother, spoke with her mother, and everybody around her seemed to notice her. Many Smiles moved around the crowd and looked for other outgoing people. No one was sitting behind the fire, so Seagull would not have to turn her body to tell her story. She lifted two large rattles, and started to shake them. "We—Ya!" Many Smiles responded from the back of the gathering. "We—Ya!"

"Shall I tell the story of how I broke my leg? Or shall I tell the story of how Seagull learned to fly? You see, the ancient ones, Míkmwesúk, as everyone knows, are the tiny people who live at the point of the land and sea. When Our People were waking and the world was new, the Míkmwesúk met together and said, 'These people are big. They will be useful to us. Let's become their friends and give them our knowledge and our love.'

"The Míkmwesúk are very, *very* small people. I would like all the children to stand up please."

All the children stood.

"This is a wonderful girl!" Seagull declared, pointing to the small girl Many Smiles had noticed when the people were coming into the storytelling circle. The girl enjoyed the attention she was getting. "You all are such wonderful children! And you know, if you look at this girl's foot—please wiggle your foot." The girl hopped in a circle and wiggled her foot so everyone could see. Everyone laughed. This laughter made the girl happy. "The tallest Míkmwesúk would have to stand on tiptoe to touch her knee—that's how small the Míkmwesúk were.

"All right, please stop hopping. Because, my dear, I have to ask you to do me a favor, and while I tell the story, Many Smiles will dance with you around the edge of the crowd. This way, everyone will be able to see exactly how tall Míkmwesúk were."

Many Smiles took the girl's hand and danced with her. She was nervous, but Many Smiles made a silly face, and everybody laughed. So the tiny girl laughed too. They danced together, and Seagull shook her rattles and sang,

> We, the tiny Míkmwesúk, will teach The People wonderful things.
> We, the tiny Míkmwesúk will teach The People to build canoes.
> We, the tiny Míkmwesúk, will teach The People to do what?

Many Smiles stopped dancing in front of one of the energetic girls he had seen enter the storytelling circle. "What will we teach you, Tall One?" The girl smiled. She understood the game.

"Teach me how to make a bowl."

Seagull shook her rattles.

> *We, the tiny Míkmwesúk, will teach The People to make good bowls.*

Many Smiles invited the girl to come and dance with them. Many Smiles made the girl do a "bowl-making dance." He pretended to be carving out the coals from a burnt burl of a tree root. They danced through the crowd.

> *We, the tiny Míkmwesúk, will teach The People, to do what?*

He stopped in front of a man who had been very talkative before the story had begun.

"To make a spear!"

Many Smiles showed the man how to dance a spear-straightening dance, and invited him to join them. The three danced and once again, Many Smiles stopped.

> *We, the tiny Míkmwesúk, will teach The People to do what?*

Soon he had many people standing, dancing through the crowd, some hunting, some making a fire, some making different shirts out of hide, and dancing many other skills.

As Seagull shook her rattles, she said, "Now everyone please stand, and dance with these people. Each of you show me a skill that was taught to The People." She shook the rattles faster and faster, until the people could no longer keep up, and gave up, laughing.

> *We, the tiny Míkmwesúk, will teach The People how to rest after their work.*

She asked everyone to sit.

"Now the tiny Míkmwesúk were wonderful Storytellers. And very often the clouds came to the earth to listen to their stories. The Míkmwesúk and the clouds became good friends. But when the clouds came and sat, they were big and cold and wet, and the tiny Míkmwesúk could not start their fires very well. So the clouds could not hear their best stories, the ones that require a proper fire. Neither could they listen to their beautiful high-voiced songs, the songs that required a proper fire. Walking Goose, the Chief of the Míkmwesúk had an idea:

We, the tiny Míkmwesúk, will teach The People to fly!

"This way, The People could travel to the sky and tell the stories to the clouds. 'Certainly, human voices are loud, so they can tell our stories to the big clouds,' Chief Walking Goose said.

"But before they could teach anyone, they received some good news: the daughter of the Chief of the Clouds and the son of Chief Walking Goose decided that they should marry. The Cloud People came down to the ground to celebrate. They stayed for many days. So many clouds came to the celebration that it was very difficult for Our People, to see anything.

"For a whole moon, the Cloud Tribe celebrated on the ground. Our people came and complained.

"'We cannot hunt, we cannot gather, we can't even start a fire because the air is so wet. When will the celebration end?' Walking Goose felt a little annoyed. First, The People did not bring gifts. Second, they didn't show the proper respect. Third, and maybe worst of all, they were right. The celebration needed to end.

"The tiny Míkmwesúk and their friends, the clouds, stirred up a storm and made the trip home very uncomfortable, to punish their insolence. The newly married couple went to live on a mountain top. The clouds and the tiny Míkmwesúk often visited the happy couple. Soon, their children were born. The children were gray and white and sometimes even black, just like The Cloud People. But they had the golden eyes and golden mouth of the tiny Míkmwesúk. They spoke the language of the Míkmwesúk. And when the children were old enough, the tiny Míkmwesúk taught them how to fly instead of giving the flying lessons to the humans who had been so impolite at the wedding."

Many Smiles walked behind the fire and lifted a long pole into the air. On the end of the pole, hanging from a string, was a wooden seagull with birchbark wings. Many Smiles made the seagull dance over the people.

"And when we see Seagull, who is the child of the clouds and of the Míkmwesúk, we know that it still speaks the language of the Tiny Ones, and in that language it tells wonderful stories to The Cloud People. With time, other seagulls were born."

Little Hawk and Dancing Rain lifted poles that were also stored outside the storytelling circle and let seagulls fly over the crowd.

"I am called Seagull. But I cannot fly. I cannot dance because I am injured. But you, who have no broken wings, I ask you to spread your wings now. You, who are My Relatives, I ask you to raise your voices to the clouds."

She made a sound like the Seagull, and she called on everyone to imitate the sound.

"And now, I would like to see each one of you, face-to-face. Fly close to me, my people, as you dance in flight around the fire. Fly close to me, so I can see each of your faces, My Relatives."

Many Smiles helped everyone to stand and to form a large circle. On the piece of drift wood, where she could reach them, Seagull had hung baskets of rattles. She began to shake one of her rattles in the rhythm of a heartbeat. Many feet formed a circle and danced around the fire. One by one they came close to her. To some, who looked brave, she called to them like a seagull, and told them to sing the seagull song as they danced. To the shy ones, she gave the loudest rattles.

Without moving off her chair, Seagull succeeded in seeing every one of the many people face-to-face. Little Hawk and Dancing Rain held the poles and made the seagulls dance. The people circled the fire seven times. The seventh time, Many Smiles directed everyone to dance close to Seagull again. Each of the participants who had a rattle gave it back to Seagull.

The dance was over. Seagull had not moved from her seat, but she had filled the room with love, and every one of those people had been seated in the shadow of her story.

4.4 The Turkey Vulture Feather:
Telling the Truth

Little Hawk visited the wigwam of Many Smiles and Seagull. Grandmother Dancing Rain came as well. "This is a difficult time. You will have to leave with the fifty-three before Seagull is well enough to travel. This means that she will be with us, and her mother and brothers this winter."

"Becomes Unseen has explained this to me. He is our chief. We do not object. But what is this about Seagull's mother and brothers? Will she not also be with her father?"

"Howling Wolf has decided to go with you, Many Smiles, and to serve as Puoin through the hard winter. He had the idea by listening to the story that we told at the gathering. He has a lesson about telling a healing story that he wishes to pass on to you."

"I know my wife will be well taken care of. Seagull's brothers are good hunters, as is her mother. By the time Seagull is healed, you should have plenty of supplies to last the long winter months. I will miss all of you, but I will send my spirit of love far over the land to be with you."

"I come to invite you to eat with us and learn another lesson," Little Hawk said. "Come before sunset this evening."

The evening arrived, and Little Hawk and Dancing Rain smiled as Seagull was helped into the wigwam by her husband.

"This evening, I will tell you a story, my grandchildren," Little Hawk said. "Grandmother Rock once taught The People to *call and respond*, to listen to a sound of Mother Earth, then to sing it, and to invite others to answer."

Long ago, when First Child came to Grandmother Rock, she told all the stories that ever were.

"Grandmother Rock," *asked First Child,* "how can I possibly remember stories you tell me? They are all the stories in the world."

"I will teach you how to call and respond," *Grandmother Rock said.* "Then you listen to me wherever I am and all you will have to do is respond."

"So how do I call and respond?" *First Child asked.*

Remember, this was at a time when the world was so new that nothing said had ever been repeated.. So Grandmother Rock called to the members of The Winged Nation and asked them to sing a song, and she sang back. Then, she called to the members of The Cloud Tribe to move their bodies and clap their hands. And when they did that, she repeated what they had done. The wolves came and sang their new songs and Grandmother Rock repeated those songs. Then, she invited First Child to sing the songs of the Two-Leggeds. The child did not have a strong voice yet, and Grandmother Rock had a hard time hearing the melodies, but she did her best to repeat them. Thus, echoes were born. A human does not have the voice of thunder, or the sound of a wolf, or the piercing cries and music of the birds. A young voice can be very quiet.

Remember, Grandmother Rock was very, very large. In fact, she was like a mountain. It took half-a-day's journey to travel across her face.

"It is hard for someone as large as me to hear creatures as small as you," *Grandmother Rock said.* "That is why some of the smallest creatures with the quietest, highest-pitched voices live close to my ear, so that I can repeat what they say. If you want to learn call and respond, you must make the journey to my ear and there you will sing and I will respond. Once you've learned how to do this, others will sing and you will respond."

So First Child went in search of Grandmother Rock's ears. Only the small creatures whose sounds were silent or near silent knew where these ears were. A chipmunk's path led to a hole. The tiny creature made many scratching sounds by chewing on pine cones. The sounds were very pleasant. First Child took a stick and scratched it against some pine cones. This made a sound like the chipmunk had made. But Grandmother Rock did not respond.

"I must still be far from her ears," *First Child said to the chipmunk and continued to follow the quiet animals.*

The mountain path led to a beaver who slapped the water with his flat tail. First Child made a clapping sound to imitate the beaver. Next, near some hollow plants, First Child listened to the breeze and repeated the plant's music by blowing into hollow stalks. These flutes made a beautiful musical sound.

Grandmother Rock still did not respond to the clapping or the flute music. "I must be very far from Grandmother Rock's ear," *First Child thought. The path continued up the mountain to a place filled with the chirping and creaking of insects. By pushing thumb hard against forefinger, and rubbing the two to-gether, First Child was able to make a creaking sound. Together, clever fingers and insects played their music.*

First Child continued the journey. In a shallow pond, Grandfather Bullfrog croaked an endless love song to his beautiful, warty, brown wife. First Child practiced making the same throaty sounds, perfecting them in order to teach the Two-Legged Nation how to croak a love song just as beautiful.

As Bullfrog was croaking the sixty-third verse, the loveliest verse of all, a flock of birds came darting through the darkening sky. These birds did not sing with loud music the way their winged brothers did. They did not Woo Hoo like the owl. They spoke very quietly, and in very high-pitched voices. In fact, their song was like the sound water makes in the springtime when ice melts and drips into puddles. By keeping teeth clenched, and opening and closing wet lips, First Child could make a similar sound, but it was so quiet. If Grandmother Rock truly responded to the sound of the small creatures, they had to live very close to her ear. First Child watched and saw the direction these strange birds were com-ing from. And as the Sun set, they seemed to be saying, 'Follow us! We'll show you the way!'

First Child had to climb, and the going was dangerous. Twice, a misstep nearly caused a terrible fall. Then, finally, nearly at the top of Grandmother Rock, First Child noticed a ledge that cast a shadow on the rocks below. Just above the ledge was an opening as tall as a wigwam, within the rock. Inside, a dark space held its secrets. From above, the sound of unfamiliar, nocturnal birds could be heard, and their silhouettes were barely visible as they hung upside-down from the formations overhead.

First Child stood in the cave and called to Grandmother Rock. First Child sang the songs of the Two-Leggeds, and Grandmother Rock echoed them back.

"You have listened to the animals and you have responded to their call. These little ones, which are called bats, have led you to my ears. I have many ears, and they are good places for you to play the music you have learned from the animals."

"But Grandmother Rock, is it right for me to slap my tail like a beaver if I'm not a beaver? Is it right for me to scratch the pine cones though I'm not a chipmunk? Should I mimic the sounds of the other creatures? Is this re-ally telling the truth?"

"Child, with your human voice and your human hands you repeated the message of the plants and animals. The truth is in the listening. Listen and repeat what you hear in the best way that you can. In the same way, feelings will come from inside of you. Repeat these feelings with your words, with your song, or with your movement. These things are the truth."

Little Hawk smiled at his students. "Many Smiles, I have a gift for you that I have been saving many years. It is a story of a young boy and a Storyteller. The young boy came to that Storyteller and said, 'Storyteller, Storyteller, Storyteller!'"

"And the Storyteller said, 'Young man, young man, young man!'"

Many Smiles laughed.

"And the boy gave the Storyteller a wonderful gift. Behind his ear, he held the feather of the vulture."

Grandmother Dancing Rain carefully unwrapped the special package. Inside, was the same turkey vulture feather that was perched behind Startle Drumming's ear when he decided to become a Storyteller. She handed it to Many Smiles.

Many Smiles twirled the feather in his hands. "My hands were so small, and this feather was so big when I took it from the stream. My grandfather taught me to stay still and listen. If he did not teach me this lesson, the feather would have drifted by me. I would have had nothing to give you, and I do not know if I would have dared to say that I wished to be Story-teller. What this feather taught me is that when our eyes are filled with tears thinking about what we do not have, we may not see that which is floating in the river in front of us. When our ears are filled with the sound of our own lament, we may miss the wise voice that has a solution for us. This is the story and the wisdom of this feather. I haven't thought about it in many years."

Little Hawk looked from Many Smiles to Seagull. "I return the turkey vulture feather to you. As you see, I have tied it to a thread. Hold the feather in front of you. When the feather moves, say what is in your heart without fear. Continue to speak your heart quietly to the feather until it stirs again."

The next day, Many Smiles and Seagull woke before dawn, and Many Smiles insisted on carrying Seagull to Eastern Rock so they could watch the sunrise together. In the heat of the afternoon, when all the world was still and even the dogs were sleeping, Many Smiles and Seagull performed the exercise exactly as Little Hawk had instructed. Many Smiles found that there were certain things that were difficult to say out loud, even to the feather. Later, Grandmother Dancing Rain came to their wigwam.

"It is time to speak what you said to the feather to each other. Listen to each other the way you would listen to the sounds of the beavers, the chipmunks, and the bats. After you have listened to each other, practice repeating what the other has said."

After each spoke, Seagull and Many Smiles realized that their friendship could survive even the words that seemed coarse, and the truth lifted the understanding between them.

Many Smiles realized that as a Storyteller, when he repeated the song of the blue jay, his heart was always open because there was no reason to fear the meaning of the song. He could focus on the sound and the feeling of the bird's call until he *became* the bird. But when he tried to repeat the truths Seagull spoke, sometimes hesitation closed his heart. When that happened, he might still be able to mimic her, but never to *become* her.

That night, before the storytelling, Many Smiles shared his thoughts with Little Hawk.

"Grandchild, it is clear. The Storyteller must become his characters and to do this, he must accept their truths with an open heart. The people listen both with their ears and with open hearts. They can sense hesitation. I know my heart must always be as open to the people as their hearts are to me. Only then do they feel that they hear the truth. Only then do I *become* my story. Tonight you will see what I mean."

That night, a young boy sat close to the fire with his grandmother. The boy was very energetic. Although he tried to sit still, the gathering made him squirm and bounce with delight. His grandmother tried to keep him still, to no avail. Grandmother Dancing Rain noticed and passed a flower to Little Hawk. The flower was cleverly crafted from a pine cone and painted red.

Little Hawk walked over to the grandmother and little boy. He crouched near the boy and then sat in front of him. The boy squirmed. Little Hawk squirmed. The boy smiled. Little Hawk smiled. The boy laughed. Little Hawk laughed. He pointed to the boy, and then back to himself. "Do you know, Grandson, that I also have a Grandmother?"

Little Hawk whispered to the boy. "She is in my heart, and she is in my memories. I always loved being with Grandmother. I am still with her in my memories."

The boy looked at his grandmother, then back at Little Hawk.

"I am *little* Little Hawk. I am five winters old!" Grandfather declared, jokingly holding up three fingers.

The boy laughed.

"It is a beautiful spring day. I am in Grandmother's wigwam. Outside, I hear a noise like a loud buzzing. It goes by one way." Little Hawk made the sounds of the buzzing.

"It goes by the other way, and makes another buzzing sound." The boy laughed as Little Hawk's head followed the buzzing sound going by in the other direction.

"Do you see what's making the buzzing sound? Let's look together. What do we see? It is not a bee. It's bigger than a bee. And it has a beautiful, beautiful coat of green and red and white."

"It's a hummingbird!" the boy shouted.

"Yes!" said Little Hawk, pointing to an invisible hummingbird zipping to and fro in the air. "Let's pretend it's early morning. The Sun is shining brightly and it has rained during the night, so that everything sparkles with water. Now, imagine me, *little* Little Hawk. That's not hard to pretend. I'm right here! But, oh, oh, oh, no! I have made a mistake. Last night, I was eating some ash cakes with maple sugar. I just loooove ash cakes with maple sugar. My grandmother had asked me to bring my bowl down to the stream, but I left it in front of the wigwam. The bowl is now filled with water from last night's rain. And what can we see?" Little Hawk pointed toward the fire. "See, right there, there's my bowl! And look, who are those animals drinking sugary water from my bowl?"

The boy looked at Little Hawk. Little Hawk pointed his finger into the air, all around, mimicking the flight of the hummingbird, and finally pointing to resting place on the invisible bowl.

"It's a raccoon!" Little Hawk declared. The boy rocked with laughter.

"No! Raccoons don't fly," said the boy.

Little Hawk frowned. "You're right. They don't. They must be walruses."

The boy laughed even louder. "They're hummingbirds!" The boy pointed to the invisible birds.

"Oh, you must be right! So, very slowly I approached the bowl, because I knew that any sudden movement would send the hummingbirds flying away as fast as they could go. Their little wings were moving so fast, the green and yellow colors of their feathers mixed together and looked like a little rainbow that was alive and laughing. Their long beaks looked like tiny sewing needles as they sipped the sweet drink. I stood there as still and as quiet as a tree with a great big smile on my face. Can you show everyone how a boy would stand quiet as a tree with a big smile on his face?" The boy demonstrated, and the people all smiled.

"All of a sudden, those hummingbirds seemed to disappear. Grandmother had just come out of the wigwam and her movement frightened the birds away. Very excitedly I said, 'Grandmother, Grandmother, two hummingbirds were sipping the sweet water from the bowl that I left, and I'm sorry that I left it, but I'm also not sorry that I left it because the hummingbirds were there and if I had not left the bowl, they would not have been there.'

"Grandmother said, 'I knew the bowl was there, but I did not know the hummingbirds were there, Loved One,' that's what she sometimes called me, Loved One.

"Grandmother continued, saying, 'I am happy that it was hummingbirds that chose to visit your bowl and not bears. You know, wherever there is sweetness, there the hummingbird will be. After you have finished cleaning your bowl, washed yourself in the stream, and have had something to eat, I will show you another way to feed the hummingbirds. Would you like that?'

"What do you think I said?"

Imagining *little* Little Hawk's reaction, the boy said, "Oh yes, yes I would like that, I would Grandmother, I would."

Little Hawk smiled. "That's just what I said! 'Oh yes, yes I would like that, I would Grandmother, I would.'" Little Hawk looked at the boy. "Are you sure you weren't there when I was five?" The child laughed.

"Well, I am very excited about Grandmother's words to me, aren't you? Five-year-old boys never know exactly what to expect from their grandmothers, but what we do know is that our grandmothers are very wise. Learning something new from Grandmother is so much fun, isn't it? It's the same way with my grandfather, always fun."

"Like you," the boy said. "Fun!" Little Hawk laughed.

"I was so excited cleaning my bowl that I forgot to wash it on the outside. So I ran back to the stream to finish the job, and I noticed that Grandmother and Grandfather's bowls were there too. I washed myself in the stream, cleaned the bowls, and brought them back to the wigwam. I filled Grandfather's bowl with food and brought it to him. He sat just outside the wigwam and waited for Grandmother, who had made ash cakes. I filled her bowl with food and held it until she sat, and then I filled my own bowl.

"I started eating so fast that Grandmother asked me, 'Are you angry at your food?'

"I answered, 'No Grandmother, I am not angry at my food.'

"'Then eat your food with respect,' she said. I knew she wanted me to remember what I was taught about eating food, to think about where the food comes from, how it comes to be in the bowl, and how it helps the body to grow and get stronger. Thinking of those things made me slow down and taste how really good my food was.

"I washed the dishes, then I ran back to the wigwam. Grandmother pulled on her moccasins and into the forest we went."

Little Hawk led the boy and his grandmother around the fire, pointing to things as he went. He walked next to the little boy, walking with a little-boy bounce in his step.

"Grandmother and I walked on the well-traveled path behind the wigwam that led to the stream that marked the beginning of a wide-open meadow. The meadow was filled with blackberry bushes, elm trees, wild strawberries, big round flower bushes, and tall grass. There were so many flowers in the meadow that the air always smelled sweet.

"Grandmother led me to one of the roundest and biggest flower bushes in the meadow. She picked a stick, pushed it into the bush, moving the branches aside until there was an opening big enough to crawl inside of the bush. 'The opening is now big enough, in you go.' I crawled inside the bush and Grandmother followed. There we sat inside the roundest and biggest flower bush in the meadow. I said, 'Grandmother, this is like being inside of a wigwam, a flower-bush wigwam.' We looked at each other and laughed.

"I asked, 'Grandmother, what about showing me another way of feeding the hummingbirds?' Grandmother answered, 'I want you to do exactly as I do.' She picked one of the brightest, longest flowers off the bush, making sure some of the stem was still attached to the flower. The stem was about half as long as my foot. The flower was shaped like a tiny upside-down wigwam and it was the brightest red there ever was.

"Grandmother took some plant cordage and tied the flower stem to a dry stick as long as my foot. She placed the stick with the flower on it between her teeth and lips, made an opening in the bush with the stick until there was a space to the outside big enough for her face to fit in. The flower on the stick in her mouth reached to the outside of the bush.

"It looked just like all the other flowers living there. She said to me, 'Now it's your turn to do what I did.' I picked one of the largest red flowers, making sure to break it at the stem to the correct length. Grandmother gave me some cordage. I tied the flower to a sassafras stick, and placed the stick into my mouth. I made a space from the inside of the bush big enough for my face so the flower would reach the outside to look like all the other flowers living there.

"We sat and waited. It seemed like a long time to me. I talked with the flower in my mouth and asked, 'When will the hummingbirds come to our flowers, Grandmother?'" Little Hawk kept his head still and moved his eyes, and spoke through his teeth, as if holding the stick. The people laughed.

"Grandmother said, 'The hummingbirds have many flowers to visit. You must be patient and quiet and they will come.'

"Suddenly I heard the wings of the hummingbird. First one, then three, now there were four hummingbirds, going from flower to flower right in front of me! I stayed very quiet and my eyes followed their every move. One of the hummingbirds moved to the flower in my mouth and put its long, straw-like beak into the flower and started eating the nectar. Its wings were humming their song, and I thought it was one of the most beautiful songs I had ever heard. The hummingbird was so close and unafraid when it came to my flower, I just knew we had become friends. In my joy and excitement, my head moved, and the hummingbirds flew away.

"I turned to Grandmother and in a happy and loud voice said, 'It was right there Grandmother, right there, right there,' as I pointed to a place just beyond the tip of my nose."

Little Hawk pointed to the tip of the boy's nose and then to his own nose. He crossed his eyes as his finger pointed.

"I said, 'The little hummingbird is my new friend, Grandmother, I have a hummingbird friend!'

"'That's right,' said Grandmother. 'Paying close attention to animals and learning their ways will always give you the chance to make them your friends.'

"But you know what else I learned? That being nice to your grand-mother and learning her ways will help you learn the ways of the animals a lot faster. Now, every time I see a hummingbird, I hear my grandmother's voice, and I see her smile. I learned that day that if I sit still and listen to my elders, good things will come to me.

"When we returned home I told everyone in the family about feeding my new friend. As I went to bed that night, thinking of that day's treat, I still could hear my little friends' hummingbird wings, and they hummed me right to sleep."

The storytelling was now over. The Moon shone brilliantly and the stars were bright. The fire that had glowed so warmly during the storytelling had now been banked, and its thin, steady smoke climbed an invisible ladder of heat into the sky. Moments ago could be heard the sounds of laughter, drumming and flute playing. Now the singing of the water toads, the storytelling circle of the crickets, and the hearth fires of the lightning bugs filled the air. All the rattles and drums, the flutes and the many gifts had all been packed away.

Grandfather sprinkled seeds over the area of the circle and beyond. He sprinkled water, drop by drop, along the outskirts of the gathering and scattered some of the cold ashes and charcoal.

"Grandfather, I have often seen the elders placing gifts of tobacco in the circle where ceremony and dance and stories take place. But you also place some of these gifts to the Earth *outside* the circle."

"Grandson Many Smiles, we set aside the circle to spend a special time in the way of Our Ancestors, and our behavior inside the circle is full of reverence and respect. But what of the area outside the circle? The whole Earth must be shown respect."

Little Hawk and Dancing Rain began softly chanting a song of gratitude to the Great Spirit. Little Hawk looked toward the starry sky to the South. The South was a place of warmth and plenty. Little Hawk thought about all the good things that happened during the storytelling. "Focusing on the little boy was a good thing. All the listeners seemed more relaxed, especially the young children who were sitting with their grandparents. I think that worked very well. It was wise of you to pass me the flower."

"The boy reminded me of a hummingbird," Dancing Rain said. "You told the story very well. I am glad the boy was restless with his grandmother, he made an excellent focal point for all the listeners." Dancing Rain and Little Hawk sat silently together for some time.

Grandfather looked to the stars in the Northern Sky, where cold winds can sometimes teach the lessons. "Perhaps the other children were not involved enough in the story. Maybe I focused too much on only the one."

"I agree," said Dancing Rain.

Grandmother looked to the Western Sky, the sky that the Sun and the Moon travel toward, and she thought about storytellings yet to come. She said, "I think that when we tell that story next time, we should ask all the children to stand and to move their arms very, very quickly, like hummingbirds. Especially those twitchy boys and girls who have not learned to sit still. They can use their energy to help us tell the story."

Little Hawk thought about this.

"Hmm…have the children stand and flap their arms quickly, like hummingbirds. Perhaps we can also include some rattles that sound like hummingbird wings."

Little Hawk looked towards the East, where the life-giving Sun originates like an ancestor. "Our grandmother joined us today, it was good Dancing Rain, that you reminded me of a story that honored our grandmother, and therefore reminded the boy to honor his grandmother. The ancestors were pleased."

Many Smiles looked in the four directions of night sky. Soon, he would leave Seagull and Little Hawk and Dancing Rain and travel with his uncle as Storyteller to the winter camp.

Am I ready? How will I do without my wife and Caretaker? And how will I do without my teachers?

Then Many Smiles realized that Little Hawk and Dancing Rain had already answered that question. Even when he became a grandfather himself, he would always have teachers—people who spoke like the raw North Wind—telling him how he could improve next time. He would have people who spoke like a soft Southern Rain, full of warmth and praise for what he had done correctly. And he would have the guidance of the ancestors and the children yet to be born, teachers of the East and West, the guidance of ancient traditions, and the guidance of new lessons yet to be discovered.

The restless boy and Little Hawk's grandmother had both been teachers that evening.

The four Storytellers sat and reflected on the lessons they had learned. They sat in silence, and listened to what the silence had to tell them.

4.5 A Story of Understanding:
Storytelling for Difficult Times

Seven mornings after the gathering, the winter camps were established. Many Smiles and his father-in-law, Howling Wolf, lived near Becomes Unseen's wigwam with Talking Leaves, the Keeper of the Fire. The other wigwams were spread far apart on the land. Families traveled, tracked, hunted, and visited. In the new territory where Becomes Unseen was Chief, Many Smiles was sometimes called upon to help Howling Wolf, the Puoin, tend to The People of the new village. "Storytelling can help lift The People's spirits in difficult times, Many Smiles. There is a type of story I sometimes use that I call *A Story of Understanding*. I hope you will be able to observe this type of storytelling under happy circumstances this winter."

The wind sang and the snow quietly listened, falling as the Moving Lights of Many Colors danced in the Northern Sky. One day, Little Bow came running into camp. "My son, Sea Mink has been burned. Please help him."

"How bad is the burn?" asked Howling Wolf.

"We were making birch tar. The tar splashed on Sea Mink's right arm and fingers. It burst into flame. Now he cannot use his hand and is too sad to eat."

"How long ago did it happen?"

"Four days ago. At first, the wounds did not look so bad. But they got worse. Sea Mink will not speak of it and he pushes his food away."

"Do you have enough room for two visitors?" the Puoin asked.

"We would welcome a visit. I have asked Sea Mink and some of the others to build a separate wigwam so that you could come. Hunting has been good. We have laid in many supplies. We plan to send a large toboggan with extra meat to help feed any of the others who might need food."

"Building a separate wigwam for us is a good thing. That shows Sea Mink he can still be useful, even with one hand. A task helps to remove the focus from the injury," Howling Wolf said.

When Many Smiles and his father-in-law arrived at Little Bow's camp, Howling Wolf examined Sea Mink's wound. The burn was large and it had badly damaged the fingers of Sea Mink's dominant hand.

"I want everything to be as it was, Grandfather Puoin. I want you to make my hand work again. I don't understand why this happened. How can I be of use to my people with only one good hand?"

"Do you wish to understand, Sea Mink?" Howling Wolf's voice was firm.

"Yes. Please help me."

Howling Wolf spoke privately to Many Smiles. "Those who lose much movement in this way need exercise. The more Sea Mink's body moves, the quicker he will heal. We must keep reminding him that it is good to understand why this happened."

The next morning, Howling Wolf drank some warm, pine needle tea with his son-in-law. "Many Smiles, it is time for you to teach Sea Mink how to tell the story of what happened to him. You must create a character, so Sea Mink can transfer what he has suffered onto the character. You must tell the story and then encourage Sea Mink to tell the story many, many times."

"I will do as you ask, Father. Is it the Story of Understanding?"

Howling Wolf smiled at his son-in-law. "You will see."

Many Smiles knew that if he told the story and used a Wiklatmu'j as his character, the little crow-like people would not object as long as he left a gift for them. So he began his story.

"The little people had gathered much birchbark. Wiklatmu'j Wind Storm made the tar carefully in a small oven and gathered the resin to use to glue her spear points to their shafts. But one batch, a particularly large batch, got too hot. It changed to oil. As Wiklatmu'j Wind Storm was pouring the oil into a birchbark container, she got too close to the fire. The oil caught fire, the container caught fire, and she shook and flapped her hands like a bird. Immediately, the oil splashed onto her arm and fingers, and burned her until she could not use her right hand. She hollered and ran out of the wigwam and dove into the snow, rolling and rolling and rolling, and yelling again and again with pain. Her father lifted her out of the snow, held her in his arms, and calmed her down.

"Now I will tell the story again," said Many Smiles.

"This small Wiklatmu'j was making birchbark tar. Soon the smell of it was overpowering in the small wigwam. It was making her dizzy. She wanted to finish making the tar quickly so the smoke would leave the wigwam. She put all the birchbark into the clay oven and added extra coals."

Many Smiles' arms and legs moved and danced. His movements made Sea Mink smile.

"Now the Puoin tells me that you must tell the same story, and tell it several times. Tell it with movement, with dance, with voice."

Sea Mink did as he was told. Each time Sea Mink told the story, he focused a little bit more on the details of the injury, and less on the pain itself.

"It is good what you have done," Howling Wolf told Many Smiles.

That afternoon, Sea Mink's appetite returned and he had something to eat. After eating, Howling Wolf sent Sea Mink to the new wigwam to rest and be all alone.

"It is important that Sea Mink spends time alone. Quiet time will help him think clearly. He needs to tell the story by himself, to breathe by himself, to dance by himself, to hear his voice alone. He must come to see for himself that the injury had a purpose."

When Many Smiles visited Sea Mink again the young man was silent. The wind whistled outside the wigwam, and Many Smiles noticed how well the shelter had been built.

Finally, Sea Mink spoke. "What must I do now? I might never use my right hand again. I will be useless to my people."

"Your hand will not be the same as it was, but whether this makes you useless is your decision to make. Now tell me. Can you imagine that you will feel unhappy forever? Can you imagine someday that you might smile again?"

Sea Mink answered, "Perhaps, some day, such a day will come."

"Then why not make that day of future happiness today?" said Many Smiles.

"And this fire spoke," Many Smiles said, "and it leapt and danced and said, 'I ask you forgiveness for consuming your skin.'"

Sea Mink stared into the fire. "Fire, you have cooked our food and heated our water. My own impatience caused a moment's lack of respect for you. It is a lesson that I will not forget."

Sea Mink was asked to forgive the birchbark tar and the wood fuel.

"Have you forgiven everything and everyone for your burn?"

"My people, I am responsible. I never had anyone to forgive."

A few weeks later, Sea Mink and Little Bow came to the Puoin's camp. Sea Mink thanked Many Smiles and Howling Wolf.

"I want to thank you both. As you see, the hunt has been good and we are glad to express our gratitude by sharing these gifts with you. I also have a special gift for the Puoin and the Storyteller," Sea Mink said. "I want to tell you the end of the story about the Wiklatmu'j.

"One day, the Wiklatmu'j was told by her Puoin that she must find the person she blamed for what happened to her and forgive that person. She claimed that she did not blame anyone, but when she washed her hand in the waters of the Crystal Lake, she saw her own reflection, and she shouted at the reflection, 'It's your fault, you are to blame!' And then she remembered her promise to the Puoin, and she asked herself for forgiveness, and in that moment the pain stopped and the healing moved faster, both in her body and in her heart."

Sea Mink took a stick from the bundle he carried. His hand was scarred, and he could not move his fingers as he could before, but he spun the stick on a fireboard and produced a coal so quickly that all were amazed. He looked toward Talking Leaves. Talking Leaves nodded his approval.

"Grandson," Talking Leaves said, "we can all be useful in different ways. I have waited and hoped for someone I could teach all that the Keeper of the Fire must know."

"Grandfather Talking Leaves, when my hand healed enough and I discovered that I could still use a stalk to make a fire, I made fire over and over until it was easy. I realized that perhaps the fire had chosen me and that with your help, I could become Keeper of the Fire for the new village. The day that I burned my hand became a day like all the days before it, days that are filled with unexpected gifts."

After Sea Mink had told his story, Howling Wolf leaned over to his son-in-law. "Son," he said, "*that* is what I call A Story of Understanding."

Becomes Unseen's tribe lost no one that winter, The People survived, and they flourished. Fifty-three left with Becomes Unseen, and fifty-three returned. Many Smiles was anxious to find out if Seagull had been all right throughout the long winter. Eight of his wife's people had left to make their winter camp. In the springtime, Seagull had a surprise for her husband. Eight had left in Seagull's group to make winter camp, and nine returned. Many Smiles was now a father.

The new winter village had gathered many cones of maple sugar, had made many spear points, baskets, and new clothing and blankets. By the Moon of the Ripening Fruit, a decision had been made.

"I am proud of the accomplishments of our summer camp," One Moccasin said. "I understand Becomes Unseen's vision for Our People, and I would vote for him to be the chief of the new village."

"I thank you, One Moccasin," said Becomes Unseen. "I say we share the same vision for Our People. You are generous and fair, and I have grown to love and to respect you as a brother. I would vote for you to be the chief of the new village."

"I will speak," said Silver Eagle, the Chief of Little Hawk's clan. "Someday, I will go to sing in the sacred caves of the ancestors, and become a child by my father's feet. I have been chief of this village for many years, and I have asked the Great Spirit to let me live to help a new chief to lead my people. The Great Spirit has given me what I asked. We have spoken to the Clan Mother, my wife Little Dove, and she approves of this change. If it is agreeable to all, One Moccasin, I ask you to consider becoming chief of our village. The two of you, One Moccasin in our village, and Becomes Unseen in the new village, will continue your friendship and will lead Our People for many years to come. Our three villages will be a strong family, and much good will come from us all working together."

And so it was that One Moccasin and Becomes Unseen, guided by the wisdom of Silver Eagle and Little Dove, both became village chiefs.

4.6 *Helping Hands:*
Another Way to Read Stories from the Landscape

The seasons came and went, and Many Smiles and Seagull raised a daughter, Quiet Claw, and a son, Long Canoe, in the village where Becomes Unseen was chief. The village honored the ways of the ancestors, embraced the difficult lessons of the hard times, and remembered that its actions should benefit the children now, and to the seventh generation.

One morning, Long Canoe approached Many Smiles. "Father, for my whole life, the ten years I have lived, you and mother have told us stories. Now Grandfather Becomes Unseen has taught us a special way to tell a story, and we would like you both to come with us, and let us show you what we have learned."

"Ah, I think you have learned about the *story that the land tells us*, the kind that keeps us from losing our way. I know this because Uncle Becomes Unseen taught the same thing to me."

Quiet Claw spoke. "Father, we have learned to tell a *story that the land tells us*. But this is a different sort of story that is told by the land. Your uncle tells us that every track in the forest is a character in a story. Uncle has taught us how to read the language of the tracks, to understand the song of the birds, and to know what the plants have to tell us."

The family left the village. The children ran ahead and looked for tracks. In a few moments, Quiet Claw rushed back to her parents. "I searched for a story and I heard the seagulls crying instead. They have come inland. That means rain. We know that it rained last night, but the birds think it will rain again, and if the seagulls are here, it must be raining over the Great Water."

A red hawk made its presence known with its shriek-call and spread its wings. The family continued deeper into the forest. A blue jay warned the forest creatures that the Two-Leggeds were on the move and further ahead, more blue jays shouted, "We understand!"

"The blue jays think we are all the way up the trail," Long Canoe said. "That's strange. They usually know exactly where we are."

They reached a stream. Quiet Claw pointed to a tiny twig. "A child came through, just before last rain."

"How can you tell?" Many Smiles asked.

"See, the part of the tree which broke off? It's sharp. The color is still bright. Look at the ground. Where the twig fell in the sand, it made a tiny roof. See? The sand is higher underneath the twig than where the water washed sand away. The twig left its own image in the sand. But why would a twig have broken off of the tree, unless something was moving through the forest?"

"Do you have an answer?" Many Smiles asked.

"Grandfather Becomes Unseen says the stories are in the tracks. Look where these green leaves were trampled. See where the footprints of a child who was running home in the rain stepped on them, sinking them into the ground. His tracks make a leap. It looked like he just grabbed his clothes when he jumped out of the water, didn't even stop to put them on. Was he running from something? Here's his track. He digs his toe in here! You can see from this small ridge that he turned his foot sideways and twisted his body with great speed as if something startled him. I know! It was thunder! Here he takes another step, looks in the same direction. Here he puts his breechcloth back on."

Quiet Claw crouched by the stream. The mosquitoes danced over her skin. "Look at this small paw print. A marten was here. It was startled by the running boy, the toes twist in the sand. He keeps looking at something!" She pointed. "There, look, there's a fallen cedar tree. This great maple branch fell on top of it—we should move the branch and bend the tree upright again." The family moved the maple branch out of the way so that the cedar tree could grow. Long Canoe remembered where the branch was because the wood could make many useful tools.

"This maple branch was hit by lightning. Perhaps the sound made the boy jump from the water."

"Look on the deer run," Quiet Claw said. "The small plants are still wet with dew. The animals haven't come to the stream this morning."

"Our night friends did not travel far yesterday," Long Canoe said. "Tonight they'll feel very hungry. They will be acting grumpy."

"Look! These human tracks are fresh! They must have been made just before we arrived. Maybe when we heard the blue jay up the trail, it was warning the forest about the stranger who made these tracks. Here, the same person dropped some blackberries. He was definitely walking down this trail."

"Look, pine cone partly stripped, partly nibbled. It's been here just since this morning. There is another! And squirrel tracks!"

Long Canoe bent closer. "Oh, but it's a sad story for the squirrel. Look at the swept sand on the trail. The red hawk captured a young squirrel. Look, all along here are nibbled pine cones. This must be a squirrel family. That little squirrel had grown too bold. If he had listened to his father and stayed under cover, he might not have turned into a meal for the red hawk.

"Over here, the human tracks continue down the trail. See how strangely the moccasin is made! The leather has been split and repaired. Our stranger must have been walking a great distance. He is not steady on his feet, sometimes he runs, sometimes he stops, sometimes he loses his balance. He travels alone, so he isn't a hunter. Look! He has taken some ash tree boughs."

"Maybe he's making a bed," Quiet Claw guessed. "He went up the hill. Here he gathered birchbark and there he collected some more fruit. He must be preparing a home in our territory. Look! There he is! Climbing the rock! It's the stranger! If he's stumbling, we should help him."

"No," Long Canoe said sternly. "Grandfather Becomes Unseen tells Our People that if we observe a stranger we should tell the Chief before we greet the stranger. We must be cautious. Isn't that the lesson we learned from the young squirrel? He was not cautious enough."

The family returned to the village to report to the Chief. Later that evening, Many Smiles' family relaxed in their wigwam. "So now you have gathered in your basket all that you need to build a story. Will you build it for us, my children?"

"But father, didn't we do that by showing you all the footprints? Becomes Unseen says that every footprint has its own spirit, and all footprints together share a single spirit. So by telling you the story of one footprint, didn't we tell you the story of all the footprints?"

"My son, every deer hide can be a drum, but does that mean you make music by beating a deer with a drum stick? No. Once you have the deer hide, you carefully work it into a drum, or a coat, or a breechcloth, or whatever Our People wish it to become. And so it is with the stories you have gathered from the footprints. Now it is time to weave them together and create a story, and that story will teach The People what you have learned."

"We will tell the story, Father."

Then the children put together a story with a lesson and told the story to their parents. Many Smiles and Seagull felt good for the children, and over the years, every now and then, they asked their children to tell the story again.

The evening after they had gone tracking, Becomes Unseen approached the family wigwam. "Today, you acted very well. You let me know that a stranger had come to our shores. His name is Climbing Rock. He told me that he had come ashore to fix his canoe which was damaged in the storm at sea. I have brought him to see you because he is also a Storyteller. May I invite him into your wigwam?"

"Climbing Rock will sit high in our wigwam, next to the Chief," Seagull said. "Outside the wigwam, I have a hide full of stew that is hot and two clean bowls for our guests."

Climbing Rock said, "I have gathered a small portion of tobacco from your lands. I offer it to you. My own tobacco was lost in the storm that damaged my canoe. I was traveling from the South. I came in search of stories and to visit the oldest Storyteller."

"This is a kind and good man," Quiet Claw said. "Perhaps we didn't need to take such caution to welcome him."

"Child, it was proper to call for the Chief. I am kind, it is true. But I wasn't always so kind. Once, when I was little, I grew tall faster than any of my other friends. Sometimes, I acted badly toward the other children and forced them to do my work. Then my mother told me a story that Our People tell, that was very much like the story of my own life. Would you like to hear it?"

How Helping Hands Got His Name

A long, long time ago on a beautiful part of Turtle Island—way up in the Northeast, where the first rays of the Sun warms and lights up each day—lived a people known by some as the Wabanaki. Others called them People of the Dawn and People of the East, but they called themselves The People. They were just like you and me. They lived in wigwams, as we do, and it is from these people that my tribe, the Penobscot, and your tribe, the Lnúk were formed. In the eyes of people who live in the West, you and I are both Wabanaki.

In one village lived a boy who was much taller and bigger than all the children his age. He made it very difficult for the other children of the village to get along with him. When there was a game of spear and hoop, the boy would not let the other children throw at the rolling hoop.

"I must go again and again. I will tell you when you may have a turn."

(The Storyteller changed his voice so expertly that everyone laughed.)

When playing ice-stick-slide, where a long groove is made in the ice and the stick is pushed to see how far it will slide, he bumped the children so their slide was always shorter than his. When playing ball-toss he threw so hard it would hurt the other children's hands when they tried to catch it. He treated the children in a bad way, pushing them around, picking on them, saying words to make them feel bad.

Brings Hurt is the name that the other children gave to the boy who did not wish to get along.

None of the children liked him or wanted to be friends with him. He made fun of the way they looked or the way they dressed. He called them ugly, and stupid, and dumb. He made it very hard for the children to like him because of his bad ways.

He made up songs to tease them...

> *You are all so dumb and skinny*
> *You are all too weak*
> *I'll always be smarter—be stronger*
> *And cannot by you be beat*

When at home in his wigwam, no one wanted to visit because of Brings

Hurt. His mother, Healing Waters, and his father, Blue Raven, told him not to behave in that way.

"Mother—Father, I do not care what the children think of me and I am afraid of nothing," *said the boy.*

"If you had no hands to push the other children around," *his father said,* "you would know how much your hands really mean to you."

"If you had no voice to yell at them and order them around to your liking," his mother added, "you would know what it is when you cannot tell your feelings to others. We hope you learn the lesson of how to live in a good way soon. You must use your hands and voice to bring people together, not to push them away."

After Healing Waters and Blue Raven spoke to their son about his behavior toward the other children of the village, he left the wigwam with a piece of dried fish. He walked up a little hill to sit and eat his salmon. He could see the hunters of the village in canoes, fishing. The hunters were using their hands to throw the nets and spears, sometimes calling to each other, letting everyone know where the fish were. He thought to himself, "They are fishing for all the people of our village, using their hands and voices in a good way."

At that very moment, an eagle swooped down to where Brings Hurt was eating his fish. The eagle's long talons grabbed and snatched the fish from his hands. He yelled at the eagle, "Bring back my salmon! Bring back my salmon!"

(The Storyteller said this with a cry that sounded *exactly* the way Many Smiles imagined the misguided child would cry.)

"Wee-Hah for Eagle!" *Long Canoe cheered. Everyone laughed.*

It was as though the eagle never heard Brings Hurt's voice as he flew away with the fish. In the eagle's whistling cries and flapping wings, the boy thought he heard the words, "Use your hands in a good way."

At the same time this was happening, a strong wind started to blow.

(The man curved his lips and tongue and blew to make the sound of the wind blowing. It was a good effect and Many Smiles reminded himself to ask the stranger to teach him how to do that.)

The wind went rustling through the tree tops and from the wind's rustling he thought he heard the words, "In a good way! In a good way!"

The eagle and the wind must have been listening when his mother and father spoke to him and now they were saying the same thing.

That night in his bed, he was thinking about what his mother and father had said to him and what the eagle and wind had said to him.

"In a good way! In a good way."

He pulled the moose-skin blanket over himself and closed his eyes to go to sleep. But before he went to sleep, he pulled his hands from under the blanket, looked at them and said, "Ha-ha, I still have my hands and I can hear my voice, ha-ha-ha."

His tired eyes slowly closed and then he was dreaming, maybe, maybe… maybe he was dreaming. He could not pull his hands apart!! He looked down at them and they had grown together. He pulled and pulled as hard as he could, but he could not pull them apart.

He sat up quickly and the moose-skin blanket fell off him. He shivered. The night was cold. He reached to pull the blanket up to cover himself, but he could not. His hands had grown together, and he could not pull them apart or hold anything. He looked around for his mother and father, but they were not there.

So he yelled and yelled for them to come to help him, but no sound came from his mouth. He no longer had a voice and could not be heard. He was so afraid, he began shaking, and crying, and trying hard to pull his hands apart. He called for help—but still no sound came from his mouth.

He feared that now he would be picked on and called hurtful names. He wondered if the children would do to him exactly what he had done to them. He cried out again for someone to help him, but still he had no voice. His cries could not be heard so no one knew how much he was hurting and how bad he felt.

(The man moved his body so well, showing how his hands were stuck together, asking the children to help him pull them apart. Seagull smiled. This man was an excellent Storyteller.)

He heard the wind blowing outside and it seemed to be saying, "What will you do now, Brings Hurt, the boy who does not wish to get along?"

And Brings Hurt was so frightened, he began to make promises.

"If my hands ever come loose and go back to the way they were, I will not use them for pushing and shoving the other children of the village. If my voice comes back, I will use it to let other children know that name calling is not a good way to behave."

At first he was so afraid that he did not notice that his voice had come back. And he did not see that he was waving his hands around in the air while he was talking.

"My voice is back!!! My hands are apart!!!"

He was so excited and happy he yelled as loud as he could, "Mawiglulg!" This is our expression of good feelings. Say it with me. See if it brings good feelings to you.

"Mawiglulg!" *everyone said.*

The Storyteller pointed to Becomes Unseen. "Now just you, Chief. Please say it, only say it as if you were Brings Hurt."

"Mawiglulg!" *said Becomes Unseen.*

"That is good, Chief, but I think I know a way to make it better. Make your voice high and crackly, like the voice of a young man."

"Mawiglulg!" *Becomes Unseen said again. He tried to make his voice sound high and crackly. Quiet Claw and Long Canoe thought this was so funny, they leaned on each other, laughing until tears formed in the edges of their eyes.*

"Mawiglulgh! Is this funny, little ones?"

"We mean no disrespect, Grandfather Becomes Unseen, it's just that you sound so much like a boy whose voice is changing, but you look so grown up!"

"Well, there you see," *said the Storyteller laughing.* "Mawiglulg! It really does bring good feelings." *And that's exactly what Brings Hurt said. And then he swore:* "I will help, not hurt." *Over and over he repeated,* "I will help, not hurt," *as he looked at his hands.*

Blue Raven and Healing Waters were standing over him when his eyes opened, awakened by the sound of Blue Raven's voice, "What came to you in your sleep, my son? It sounded as though you were crying."

"Mother, Father, my dream, it was so real. I thought I was awake."

And, Brings Hurt described his dream.

"Do not be afraid," *his mother said.* "It was a good dream." *At last he saw how much his hands and voice really meant to him.*

Healing Waters and Blue Raven were so happy that their son had learned to be good-hearted, that they had a Naming Ceremony to give him the new name, Helping Hands. The whole story about the dream and how he had changed in a good way was told to everyone in the village during the ceremony.

From that day on, the other children never again called him Brings Hurt, the boy who did not wish to get along. He became Helping Hands, friend of all the children. And all the children became his friends, too. Now the people visited his wigwam and he was invited to sit in all of the wigwams of the village.

And whenever someone reaches their hands out to help someone else, they might not know it, but Helping Hands smiles, and says, "Mawiglulg".

We can choose to live in a bad way or to live in a good way with others. When someone new comes among your people, we can choose to welcome them and help them, the way I was welcomed. Together, we can make good things happen by helping each other—not by hurting each other. After all, we are all relatives.

That is my story, my friends. Sometimes, after telling a story, the Storyteller sings a song to celebrate the lesson of the story. This is the song for my story:

> *Good words can make someone feel better*
> *Our hands can be used to help*
> *When we see all the good they can do*
> *We see it helps us, too.*

The Storyteller's kind eyes moved from face to face.

Some people say if you listen very closely—when an eagle swoops down and catches a fish, as it is flapping its wings, rising higher and higher into the sky, and making its whistling cries—you can hear the words, "In a good way, in a good way."

And if the wind blows through the top of the trees at that same time, you may hear the words again, "In a good way, in a good way."

And we all remember how Helping Hands got his name.

> *Hear the eagle—In a good way*
> *Hear the wind—In a good way*

Hands you use—In a good way
Words you say—In a good way.

I have told my story.

Everyone in the wigwam waited, to make sure Becomes Unseen had nothing to say. As the oldest, and as the Chief, everyone waited for him to speak first.

"Climbing Rock, I thank you for the story, which I accept as a gift. Seagull has given you her wonderful soup and you have given her this story. My nephew has given you the hospitality of his wigwam, and you have given him this story. Now I give you my tobacco pouch to replace the one you lost in the storm. You have taught us a good story. As for these two children who have heard your story, you have given them a good lesson."

The children looked at each other. They knew that they had nothing to offer the stranger, but they also knew that to speak before their parents have spoken, or before the Climbing Rock responded would not be respectful, so they waited. Seagull looked at her children's faces, and noticed the worry.

"Chief Becomes Unseen, my people will learn of your generosity through the stories I tell about you and your people. I have already received a wonderful gift from the man and woman in this wigwam. Both these children have already given me a gift. You told me that tracking this morning led to my being discovered and brought me to this village. In my tribe, the children bring the food bowls back from the river, having scrubbed them."

"This is our way as well," the Chief said.

"Then I have been given a gift of respect by both these children. My bowl was very clean. I thank them both. My People, when we receive a gift, we hold our hands out, with our palms up, and then palms down. This means that we are grateful for the gift from the giver and we are grateful to the Earth which was the source of the gift."

"My brother and I will remember what you have taught us," Quiet Claw said. "We thank you for your gift that came out of your footprints. But we would like to give you something more. We would like to tell you the story of those footprints, the stories that the land always tells."

4.7 *Always the Same, Always Different:* Borrowed Stories

One winter evening, the Many Smiles' family sat together in their wigwam. "Wife, you who brings to my spirit what maple sugar brings to my taste, we have had a happy life together. We have traveled great distances. My daughter will be a Puoin. My son has become a skilled crafter of snowshoes and toboggans and canoes."

"Husband, you say that we have been happy together. You are to my spirit what the warmth of a sunny day by the Great Water is to my body. We have traveled distances and we have seen wonderful things. Our son and daughter will be helpful to our tribe."

Long Canoe listened thoughtfully. As clever as his mind was, his hands were equally skilled. When the children played games of hoop and spear, they did not challenge Long Canoe because the spears he had made always flew straight through, no matter how fast they threw the hoop. As for his sister, Quiet Claw, they never wanted her to be one of the searchers. Their tracks, the birds, the land itself would always tell Quiet Claw where the others hid. Long Canoe was good at noticing the special gifts of others. His older sister had an unusual awareness. She noticed how the camp dogs acted when a human was ill, and realized that dogs could sense illness before the Puoins themselves.

Long Canoe waited to make sure that his parents had finished saying what they wanted to say and that his sister did not wish to speak first. Then he spoke. "My Mother and my Father, you both say that you have been happy together. We have also been happy with you. You say we have traveled great distances and this is true. I remember the lesson you taught us about being useful to our people. It was the lesson of the fuel basket."

"Will you tell us the story, Canoe Builder?" Seagull smiled.

"If it pleases my parents, the Storytellers, and if my sister, the Puoin, will help."

Quiet Claw smiled. She sat higher than him in the wigwam because she was older. Now she moved back down the wigwam, toward the door, to sit beside him. When they were in the wigwam, they had to kneel so their eyes could meet the eyes of their father, who sat cross-legged, and the eyes of their mother, who sat on her feet.

Long Canoe sprang to his feet and playfully mimicked the gestures of his father. Quiet Claw pretended to play a rattle, the way she had seen her mother do it. Long Canoe's eyes moved from face to face. Seagull and Quiet Claw began to laugh.

"What's so funny?" Many Smiles asked.

"He's pretending to be you," Seagull said, "If you could see yourself tell a story, you could see that he does it just like you."

Long Canoe even spoke with his father's whispery voice. This made the women laugh again.

Seven or eight winters ago, when I was so small I had to look up to see the seed pods on a dogbane stalk, we were all together here in this winter camp, in this wigwam, in this place of the Sugar Maple Grove, the place I will always think of as my home. The basket and the leather straps we used to gather wood, sat together in their usual place inside the wigwam, just as they sit there today.

North Wind was flapping one powerful wing outside. The snow on the ground was lifted into the air and danced in circles. The snow floated above the smokehole and around the open door and rested on the snow that had already fallen. The frost on the brown oak leaves outside made beautiful ice paintings. I, Long Canoe was drawing these designs on a piece of birchbark when my mother's voice called my name.

"Stop what you're doing, wash yourself, get dressed. Make sure the basket is empty."

I became excited and began to dance. I knew what that meant, a new adventure of tracking and hunting. I rushed outside and, with a handful of snow, I rubbed my face and hands clean. I reached for a small stick of dogwood to clean my teeth. The sprigs are not only good for cleaning teeth, but they are good for making tool handles, too. This tree is home to the turkey...

Quiet Claw laughed, "Brother, your hands are good at making things and you hunt well. The dogwood has many gifts for our people. But continue with the story."

"Oh, yes! Where was I in the story?"

"You were getting cleaned up to go out with Mother."

Then Father tied wraps around my legs, covered me with a long blanket, gave me mittens, and a rabbit fur hat. Mother did the same with Quiet Claw. Then she put us in warm moccasins and tied on snowshoes. The snowshoes were made out of ash splints and rawhide, and sewn with a needle made from bone…

"Brother…"

"Oh, yes, the story!"

Well, we put on our moccasins and we tied on the snowshoes. Mother handed me the basket and older sister, Quiet Claw, the leather straps. She looked as excited as we felt to be going out into the snow.

Outside the wind had stopped. The snow was only as deep as my hand. That's how Grandfather Becomes Unseen taught me to measure how deep snow was. The snow was still deep enough to make really big tracks with my snowshoes. Grandfather has always told me to walk in tracks that are already made. They're easier to walk in. We started down the hill to a stream where the beaver had built a dam a few summers before.

"Look! There's where the stream should be. It's all covered by snow. What do you say, Mother? Should we wait here? Yes? We will wait."

I watched Mother walk down to the frozen water. She brushed off the snow. She was looking for blue and clear-colored ice. That meant it might be strong enough to walk on. Mother took a small piece of buckskin from her carrying bag, laid it on the ice, and pressed her ear to the ice.

Long Canoe demonstrated. His face pretended to show his mother's concentration. He raised an eyebrow and nodded to himself, as Seagull often did. His family laughed.

"We can cross here," *Mother called. We began to gather sticks, placing them in a pile with the leather straps beneath it. Mother would often stop what she was doing and go back to the stream and listen.* "If I hear the stream start to run, or if the color of the ice changes, we must cross quickly."

Mother always found more wood than we did. I saw many different tracks in the snow and asked my mother what had made each of those tracks. Then my sister and I followed the tracks to see where they led. We were not allowed out of our mother's sight. We were careful to do what she said. She knew how to keep us from harm.

After Mother decided we had collected enough fuel, she tied the leather straps around the long bundle of sticks. She handed my sister the basket full of small tinder and the tree mushrooms that help start a fire. The branches in the leather strap were too long for my small body to carry, but Mother carried them easily. She strapped them to her forehead and shoulders. I would look for my footsteps in the snow, following the tracks I had made that morning. I told my mother that I was tracking myself, and I was harder to track than an owl. That made her laugh.

When we returned home, Father had some hot, pine needle tea and a delicious warm stew waiting for us. He went outside and broke the fuel into pieces small enough for use. He filled the gathering basket with the wood we had collected. He sent me back and forth, many times, to the wigwam of Chief Becomes Unseen, to store the extra wood for our village.

Grandfather Becomes Unseen gave me more hot soup. As a special treat, he gave me the sweet tip of a small, spruce tree branch to nibble. As he hung my wet clothes inside on his wigwam hoops, he said, "Grandson, by going out and finding wood to burn, you are helping to keep the whole clan warm, helping dry wet clothes, to heat cooking water, to make soup, tea, and ash cakes. Finding wood might seem like a little thing, but it is really important for all of us. As long as we care for each other, The People will always be strong. Gathering wood shows that you love your people as they love you."

I thought about his words. That winter I thought of the ways I could be more useful to my people. Now each time I see the basket it reminds me that completing small acts of caring for our village prepares you for accomplishing large deeds.

He also said that because I was willing to work hard on small tasks, I could accomplish many things I set out to do. And he said I was learning a very important lesson on how to live in a good way. I was learning how to help people by making life better for all. That's when, all those many winters ago, I knew that I must find a way to be useful to my people.

"That is a good story, Brother. It has a good lesson, and you told it exactly as Father would have, with his exact voice. Now it's my turn to tell a story in our mother's voice."

"I will drum," said Long Canoe.

Quiet Claw jumped to her feet moved her hands and body just like her mother. Even Seagull recognized her own style, and laughed.

This happened longer ago than the story told by my brother. It happened such a long time ago, that many generations of May bugs have passed.

My brother was on the cradleboard, and we were traveling south, in the Great Waters, down to the land of the Maliseet. And we were going to hear some stories, and you, Mother and Father, were going to tell some stories.

"The Maliseet make beautiful birchbark baskets shaped like people. Do you remember?" Seagull asked. "In their wigwams, the people-shaped baskets sit in a circle just like…"

"I think we may be straying from the story, my Wife," Many Smiles laughed. "Please go on, my Daughter."

When we arrived, I was surprised to see a man dressed almost exactly like Great-Grandfather Little Hawk. We sat with the people and watched him tell his stories. Some of the stories sounded very familiar to me. Many people tell the same stories, each in his or her own way, but in his movement, in his tone of voice, and even in his small playful ways, this Storyteller sounded exactly like Great-Grandfather Little Hawk.

After the storytelling was over, we introduced ourselves. When we mentioned where we were from, the Storyteller said, "Surely you must have met the respected Storytellers named Little Hawk and Dancing Rain! My brother and I are their greatest students. We followed them and listened to their stories many times in our youth."

In truth, the man had done everything perfectly, dressed like Great-Grandfather Little Hawk, sounded like Great-Grandfather Little Hawk, knew the songs of Great-Grandfather Little Hawk, and could say what Great-Grandfather Little Hawk said. This Maliseet man spoke the stories not in the Maliseet way, but in the way of our people. When our family returned from that trip and stopped in the summer camp of Great-Grandfather Little Hawk and Great-Grandmother Dancing Rain, I told him about this Storyteller.

"I remember the man you describe!" *Great-Grandfather Little Hawk laughed.* "When I was traveling with Dancing Rain, he and his brother followed us during our journey. We showed him and his brother the way we told stories. Storytelling comes from the heart. Each heart has its own rhythm. We could guide him to find his own way to tell stories, but he had to waken the stories with his own heartbeat."

Many Smiles placed his hand on his daughter's cheek. "Grandfather Little Hawk always taught me that I would find stories told by other Storytellers which my heart understood. He told me that when I found these stories, I would have to ask the Storyteller for permission to tell, and I should speak the name of the Storyteller from whom I had learned the story. Once, a Storyteller came to me after we had told many stories in Lenape country. We barely spoke the same language. His ways were very different from our own, but he made me understand a very important lesson: he told me, '*All stories are never told.*'

"Grandfather Little Hawk told me that a story is just a way of lifting understanding. Each time a story is told, the people and the Storyteller understand each other better. That is why you can tell the same story hundreds of times and each time, the story will be new."

"The snow is deepening fast, Father. We have stored two moons of wood for fires in the wigwam of your uncle, Becomes Unseen. We have enough food to last until the snow is over, and we have many games to keep us busy. We have birchbark and rootlets for baskets. While we work, and while the snow falls, we would love to hear the stories of what you learned in your travels."

"Oh please, please tell us the story of your visit with the tiny, tiny woman and the world's oldest Storyteller? I love that story!"

Seagull smiled. She nodded, and looked at Many Smiles. "It's a good story to tell while I sew this robe for you." Seagull was sewing black feathers onto the shoulders of a buckskin robe.

Many Smiles leaned forward and reached for some dried cedar leaves. He threw them onto the coals of the fire.

Do you smell the smoke my children? Well, breathe deep of it, and know that whenever I smell the smoke of cedars, it reminds me of a remarkable journey I made to meet the world's oldest Storyteller.

Five

FILLING THE SPACE WITH LOVE:

The Wisdom of the Ancestors[4]

5.1 *The Oldest Storyteller: Dressing the Part*

The springtime before Seagull broke her leg, Grandfather Little Hawk and Grandmother Dancing Rain sent us on a journey toward the South and West. The journey took almost one full moon to make. Along the way, we kept hearing stories about the village of the oldest Storyteller on Earth. We reached his village at sunset and were welcomed warmly by the people of the village, whose chiefs were women. An interpreter was sent to us. The woman had a twinkle in her dark eyes. She was so small, I could have rested my elbow on her head, but her voice was big, friendly, and filled with humor. Her language was not difficult to understand. In our travels, we had learned similar words spoken by other tribes.

---

4   Refer to curriculum p.198–203

"You've come to meet our most beloved Grandfather," *she said.* "You're just in time."

Grandfather Little Hawk had often spoken of this famous and ancient Storyteller, a man who was already old when Grandfather Little Hawk's great-grandmother was a child!

The childish part of my heart thought, "When, when, when, when is there going to be a story?" *But I was now a man, so I only asked once:* "When is Great-Grandfather going to tell a story? When will I get to hear his voice?"

The woman laughed. "That is a question you can ask him yourself."

"Please, please take us to him!"

We followed the woman out of her wigwam, toward the large wigwam in the center of the village. These people lived in the same village during both the summer and winter months, grew delicious crops, and fished in a lake. As we walked along, many friendly people greeted us.

We were led to the entrance of the wigwam. "It is I, Swimming Marten. I have brought visitors who wish to hear a story."

We entered the wigwam. It had a rounded roof, unlike our wigwams. The only light was the moonlight streaming in through the smokehole.

"I will start the fire," *said Swimming Marten. In the darkness we could see the image of Great-Grandfather. The smell of buckskin and cedar was heavy and comforting. I could hear the tinkling and rattling of shells, bringing visions of the ocean to the wigwam. As the fire rose, we could see shells on the Storyteller's shirt fringe. The ancient Storyteller seemed to dance in the shadows cast by the fire. All we could see were flashes of round, white patterns on a flowing robe thick with downy feathers. I could not take my eyes off Great-Grandfather. The firelight brightened. Some hair, carefully braided, was sewn to the right sleeve of his shirt. A lock of gray hair was braided with a lock of black.*

We were so fascinated with Great-Grandfather's regalia as he sat on his platform, that it took us a long time to realize this Great-Grandfather was not a human being of flesh, but the wooden carving of a human being. What a story his garments told! On one knee of his pants was sewn a small piece of birchbark that looked like a canoe, surrounded by delicate blue jay feathers. How could this presence fill the whole room? The stories that his regalia told were all so wonderful!

"He tells everyone a different story," *the woman said*. "The way we honor our Storytellers, after they have become grandfathers and grandmothers, is to permit them to add something to Great-Grandfather's regalia."

The stars had moved in the sky by the time we left that wigwam. The Ancient One's regalia told so many stories! Somehow, the way he was dressed spoke, and told us who he was and who his people were. Seagull and I had much to discuss.

When we returned to Grandfather and Grandmother, we immediately began to work on our own regalia. Our goal was to dress two figures made of grass in special regalia. We invited people to visit our grass figures and see if our regalia told a story. You have seen our regalia. It was made lovingly. It has some playful details, and it tells the truth about who we are. It lifts the level of understanding between us and our audience.

"And many pieces can be added to show some of the Storyteller's experiences," Quiet Claw pointed out.

"Storytelling has more than one purpose, my daughter," Seagull answered.

Many Smiles continued. "The next step was to wear the regalia we had created. And when we put it on, we became…"

"…Ourselves, but something more," Seagull said.

"We became who we chose to be when we were telling stories. Grandmother always said that the wearing of appropriate regalia is a sort of call and response. The things we wear call to us when we wear them, and they help us to respond in a good way."

5.2 Carry a Lighter Burden: Emptying Your Basket

As their children grew and traveled to the wigwams of new teachers, Many Smiles and Seagull went on one of their most important journeys. They visited the district on the Southern Shore. There, one evening, they met the great-grandson of the Storyteller Little Hawk and Dancing Rain had met when they were children. He was the same man who had taught Dancing Rain the story of Carrying a Lighter Burden.

He was a small man and very ancient, but at once Seagull could sense that this man had never lost his childlike energy and sense of wonder, laughter, and generosity. He reminded Seagull of a cricket, so small, yet so full of song and dance. "I am delighted to see you. I am so happy to know you as friends. I have a gift for you! I will tell you the story that my great-grandfather told Little Hawk and Dancing Rain when they made *their* journey here. This is a story that was told to my great-grandfather by his great-grandfather. It is very simple." He sprang to his feet, hardly needing to use his walking-stick. Immediately, he passed the stick to his granddaughter, the Caretaker.

Once, a great-grandson asked his great-grandfather, "Grandfather, you have seen the many colors of the seasons. You have known hunger and feast."

(He sang the words, and used his hands as well as his voice.)

"You have gained so much experience and life has taught you so much."

(He spread his arms wide until it seemed that the whole night sky was balanced between his arms.)

"Please give me your wisdom so that I may learn. If you could return and live your life again, what would you do differently?"

He leaned in close and paused. He waited for Many Smiles and Seagull to notice that he had stopped speaking, for the flow of the world outside the story to return to their ears. His eyes were still fixed on theirs and he was smiling. He knew he held them in his silence. His hands were lifted, and his lips were parted, as if at any instant he would say something.

He leaned forward and listened, and all could see he was listening to his grandfather's words that only he could hear. Many Smiles could almost see his grandfather whisper to him. Then he leaned back toward Many Smiles and Seagull. He pointed into the night towards his 'grandfather.' More silence, more listening.

Many Smiles loved the story. This had been the first story he had ever heard, the day he became Startle Drumming. When she had told it, Dancing Rain had not used so many words. Her story had been mostly a dance, and the feeling of the dance had stayed with him his whole life. This was a new way to tell this story, so different, yet with the same lesson and the same power.

"I see you smiling, Many Smiles." He pointed in the direction of his 'grandfather.' "Can you hear him, too?" the ancient Storyteller asked.

"Tell your grandfather that this is the first story I remember hearing. It's the lesson that made me want to be a Storyteller, the lesson about carrying a lighter burden. I wanted to help my people to carry a lighter burden, and so I became a Storyteller. I smile, my friend, my relative, because all these years later, I remember. Through Grandmother Dancing Rain, I must thank your great-grandfather for giving her the story that made me a Storyteller."

"Do you hear that, Grandfather?" The Storyteller pretended that his grandfather was still there, still listening. But this *wasn't* pretending. The Storyteller could feel that his grandfather's spirit was there, and because he could feel it, Many Smiles and Seagull could feel it, too, through him. They were responding to the Storyteller's *understanding*.

"You hear, Grandfather? Many Smiles says this is the first story he remembers hearing and—and, it's the lesson that you taught Dancing Rain that made him want to become a Storyteller, and he wants to thank you, all these years later, for giving Dancing Rain the story that made him a Storyteller."

The Storyteller leaned back, toward the darkness. Then he leaned toward Many Smiles. "Grandfather wants you to tell us how Dancing Rain told the story."

Many Smiles described the way Grandmother had danced around the fire, putting down the kindling, feeling it grow heavier. He felt it was the perfect story for any Caretaker to tell, not just the Caretaker of a Storyteller, but for *anyone* who wanted to take care of his people.

The Storyteller's great-grandson said, "Grandfather wants to know if she told the rest of the story of the Lighter Burden."

"That's all I remember. I was a very small boy, hadn't even been given my boy-name. Grandmother's way was to use few words, so that we could all remember those few she *did* say. Why? Is there more to the story?"

"Ask Grandfather," he whispered. "You must speak to him in a loud voice. Say, 'Please show me the rest of the story, Grandfather.' Say it loud."

The young Caretaker handed Seagull a rattle. She and the Caretaker began to keep the rhythm, while Many Smiles chanted with the ancient Story-teller:

> *Please show me the rest of the story, Grandfather*
> *Please show me the rest of the story, Grandfather*

The aged Storyteller, who had been squatting near Many Smiles and Dancing Rain, reached out his hands and his granddaughter stopped the rhythm. She handed him a birchbark basket. The way she handed it to him, and the way they struggled to lift it, something very heavy seemed to be inside. Finally, with great effort, he turned the basket upside-down. The basket was empty.

> *And an empty basket is the greatest burden of all.*

The voice was ancient as the trees.

In the voice of a boy: "What does that mean, Grandfather?"

"When the time comes, you will understand."

In the voice of an elder, "Now, Grandfather, I finally understand. The time has come."

"Do you understand now?"

"I do. To wish for all you cannot hold, to cry for all you have lost, that is the greatest burden of all."

The elder laid his hand on Many Smiles' shoulder.

"When the time comes, you will understand."

5.3 Words Don't Need to Be Understood: Transcending Language

How sad Many Smiles and Seagull feel! What a terrible problem! The story is so good and the words are so carefully crafted. The lessons are deep and the fire is articulated to each of the words in each of the stories. The voices have been selected, practiced, and the dialogue between Seagull, the Storyteller and

Many Smiles, the Caretaker, is meant to make people laugh. And now, what are they going to do? What are they going to do?

Many Smiles and Seagull unwrapped the items they carried with them. Their regalia was beautiful, intricately cut and stitched with designs that featured the characters in the stories they were about to tell. Every smallest detail was perfected. After so many years, Many Smiles and Seagull were ready to travel again. Their children were both grown and had wigwams of their own. Their Quiet Claw had become a Puoin and Long Canoe had become a great hunter, a just man, and a likely successor to Chief Becomes Unseen.

Everything was as it should be, and spring brought warm southern breezes and early plants and blooms on the boughs to the place known as Grove of Maple Trees. The Storytellers had been waiting many years for an early spring. They were still strong enough to make a great journey North, to hear stories from the caribou hunters who lived in skin-covered wigwams and had dogs that pulled their toboggans.

The women of Grove of Maple Trees had built a beautiful canoe from ash wood splits and birchbark. The Storytellers carried with them gifts crafted by The People for those they would meet. In return, Many Smiles and Seagull would bring back new stories that the North Winds had taught these Innu, these People of the Ice.

The couple traveled many days on the Great Water and as they traveled North, they noticed how the cold weather followed them. Still, the path of the North Wind was swift, and retreated ahead of the warmer breezes from the South.

As they traveled many days on the ocean, they saw many families of whales. Some seemed very curious. Even the young whales would come close to visit the canoe. Many Smiles took a drum out of its otter skin pouch. He drummed and Seagull sang for the whales. Did the whales respond? They splashed and rocked the canoe. They jumped in the air, twisting and splashing back into the water, just far enough away not to wet the canoe. Drumming and singing, the Two-Legged Storytellers told their tales to this family of giants. Was the understanding between these whales and the humans lifted by the storytelling? Seagull believed it was, and Many Smiles agreed.

They traveled north. They sang with the owls, heard the crackling of the great ice, and came ashore amongst a herd of strong-smelling walruses. They walked toward the walruses, showing their hands, lowering their heads, averting their eyes to show they meant no harm. They told the story of the gentleness of their people.

Seagull was thankful for the journey. "Here on this shore, did our story without words and without fire lift their understanding of us and our understanding of them? I feel it did."

After many days and nights in the canoe, they reached a village of Two-Leggeds. These were the caribou hunters who lived in the Land of the Long Days. The spring had arrived, and the people were rejoicing. Many Smiles and Seagull brought gifts from their people, but their finest offering would be the stories they prepared with such care.

How sad they feel! What a terrible problem! What are they going to do? Not one of these warm, smiling people of the North speaks their language!

The elders welcomed Many Smiles and Seagull, and invited them to sleep in the hut of the Chief. The children welcomed the Storytellers with a song, and one remarkable Innu woman sang deep in her throat with two voices at once!

On the second day, the hunters returned with a feast. Many Smiles and Seagull took out their drums and began to tell a story. It was not the story whose words were *so* carefully crafted. Still, the lessons had many layers, and the new story was also good.

They told the story of their journey. Seagull sat in the canoe, on the land, and paddled to a beat. Many Smiles imitated a whale, carrying large branches in his hands, jumping and striking the branches on the ground, like the whale strikes the water. The warm, smiling faces of the people made Seagull believe that the story had lifted the understanding between them.

Then Seagull positioned her body like a walrus on the sand, and Many Smiles approached, just as he approached the strong-smelling walruses. He wrinkled his nose, fanned the air, and the people laughed. He came close, showing his hands, lowering his head, averting his eyes to show that he meant no harm. The people smiled with recognition.

Then, the Storytellers invited the people to stand. Together, everyone danced the dance of the whale. Then with their heads up and their feet and knees in the sand, everyone stood like walruses. Many Smiles and Seagull came close to the elders, lowering their heads, averting their eyes to show they meant no harm, only respect. They gave beautifully made gifts to the people.

Afterward, the Storyteller of this tribe also told his story. He used his own words, but by his movements, by his dance and by his emotion, the strangers, Many Smiles and Seagull, understood very well. Each night, the couple would tell another one of their stories with the local Storyteller, until all the stories they had come to tell were told, and all the stories they had come to listen to were also told. These people of the long days had been great teachers to Seagull and Many Smiles. They'd taught Many Smiles and Seagull that they could speak in the language of the Two-Leggeds, of the whale, of the walrus, of the wind, and the words would be understood because it is the heart, not the mouth that speaks.

On the longest day, two moons after they had arrived, they were able to understand some of their host's language. "All stories are never told," the grandfather Storyteller told Seagull and Many Smiles.

"I have heard that said before. Why is it so?" Seagull asked.

The words were not easy to explain. "Story tells Storyteller." The Storyteller said, and pointed to Many Smiles.

"Story tells Storyteller." The Storyteller said, and pointed to Seagull.

"Story tells Storyteller." He pointed to himself, and repeated it. He pointed to the dog, pointed to many people, and pointed to the sky, then pointed to the small, leather bag around Many Smiles' neck that held the storytelling stone.

"You, me, the same story. You, me different story. All different. Story tells Storyteller."

Many Smiles and Seagull left for home in the warmth of the summer, back through the great sea of walruses and whales. They were quiet for much of the journey and thought about what the Storyteller had said.

"He meant that we tell stories, and that he tells stories, but we tell the same stories."

"My husband is wise," Seagull said.

Many Smiles laughed.

"Why are you laughing, my husband?"

"Because you always tell me that I am wise just before you show me how I am incorrect. Tell me then, my dear wife, what did the Storyteller mean?"

"I think he means the Storytellers' journey through the stories we learn can be filled with life-changing choices."

"My wife is *really* wise," Many Smiles laughed. "Perhaps the Storyteller also meant that not only do the people listen to the story, but the good stories listen to all people. Listen right to the drumbeats of their hearts, right to the dance of their spirits, and listen to them and respond, so that the stories themselves may live in a good way."

On the return trip, a tide entered the Bay of the Giant Beaver and it swept the birchbark canoe toward the rocks. Many Smiles and Seagull came to shore close to their homes, near a cave. They wondered why they had never seen it before. They felt drawn to the cave, and it called to them, and they entered.

They made a small fire with great care. They took out a quiet birchbark drum, and they sat together by the fire at the end of their journey, and sang,

> *Y'Nay ha ho ne y'nay ha ho ne eey ha ho nay y'nay ha ho ne*
> *Y'Nay ha ho ne y'nay ha ho ne eey ha ho nay*
> *Then the stories age*
> *And they stay the same*
> *And they never change*
> *But they're not the same*
> *Because every day*
> *And from age to age*
> *We stay just the same*
> *But we're not the same*
> *Because stories came*
> *And that day we changed*
> *And the stories change*
> *Us—We're not the same*
> *And the stories came*

From the change we made.
Then the stories age
And they stay the same...

And as they repeated the melody, they thought they heard echoes singing their song deep within the cave. It may be so, and it may have just been echoes. But perhaps at the end of a difficult journey they had come to Glooscap's cave and what they heard wasn't echoes at all. Maybe it was the voice of Glooscap singing with them. If they had reached Glooscap's cave, they had no request to make of him. What more could they ask? Life itself had already granted them what they needed as Storytellers—to play together, to lift each others' understanding, to fill the space they shared with love, to tell the truth, and to help each other carry a lighter burden all the days of their lives.

5.4 The Turkey Vulture Feather: How to End a Story

This has been a story about a life in storytelling. And all who have read the stories and wish to use them to learn the art of storytelling, you are my grandchildren. Now you have come to our village, lived through many seasons, seen us at our councils, and watched life unfold as you listened to this story and learned to tell your own. We have asked you to sit beside us in our wigwam and learn and practice. We hope we left you slightly hungry and that your basket is not empty.

Many Smiles was no longer a young man. Seagull was still his great love. In his eyes she would always have the splendor of youth, but time had deepened the roots of their bond. The time they spent in the wigwam telling stories, the time they spent traveling together, created in them an understanding of one another that went beyond the beauty in which each beheld the other. They knew each other's spirit. As Storytellers, they welcomed all their moods, the way those who make pottery welcome clay of different colors. They put these feelings in a special, invisible basket, and they reached for them, as they would a rattle or drum, when the story called for it.

When Many Smiles first came to the wigwam of Little Hawk and Dancing Rain, Grandfather had asked both Many Smiles and Seagull to tell them stories of the day, from the time they awoke onward to the present moment. They both did so enthusiastically, every day, speaking in great detail about everything they had seen and heard.

"This is good," Dancing Rain told them after they had patiently listened to the children's long stories. "Tomorrow, you will tell us everything that has happened in your day, while balancing on your left foot. When your right foot hits the ground, you must complete your story in three words."

Another time, Dancing Rain spoke to Seagull. "Sometimes when a story teaches an important lesson, it may cause the listener's emotions to go many places, to feel a little bit angry, so they are inspired to change that which makes them feel this anger. Anger is not a bad thing to feel. Anger, silliness, despair, sleepiness, hunger, grief, and joy—you can be taken many places by the intention of a story. There is, however one emotion you never want anyone listening to you to feel."

"What's that?" Seagull asked.

Little Hawk smiled mischievously. "I will not tell you, my children. I will *show* you."

Little Hawk began to tell a story. The story got longer, and longer, and longer. Many Smiles and Seagull fidgeted, but they tried to remain attentive. Still, the story went on and on and on. Finally, the story was over.

"I will not ask you what you thought of the story," Little Hawk said. "You are too respectful to tell your elder what you might truly think, but you must know that I told the story badly on purpose."

Seagull said, "I felt exactly the way I feel when holding my breath. I was very aware of my body and was relieved when the story was over."

"*Relief.* You know you have not succeeded as a Storyteller when the people feel that emotion when the story is over—relief. The stories you tell should not leave this world from old age. It is better to leave a feast feeling slightly hungry than stuffing yourself to the feeling of illness. Leave the people wishing that you had time to tell more stories."

Now, many years later, Seagull's life became a good story. She went away from Our People to tell stories in the Spirit World, leaving those who loved her slightly hungry, wishing she had time to tell more stories. Many Smiles knew his wife's spirit, the way husbands know wives. Over their lifetime together, they had shared so many truths. That is why when Many Smiles told his stories, his Caretaker would still tend his fire from the shadows, and pass him a special invisible feeling, as if it were a rattle or drum, when the story called for it.

In the days just after her day of quiet, Many Smiles saw Seagull in a dream and they were all together again, with Dancing Rain and Little Hawk. They all were sitting together on Many Smiles' storytelling stone, which had grown as large as Grandmother Rock. First Child sat next to Many Smiles by the fire, listening, and they all watched as Seagull told her story.

Somewhere in the night, a wolf howls. Somewhere in the night, a drumbeat is faintly heard—is it a drumbeat, or can Many Smiles feel his heart beating with anticipation of what is to come? Only the fire interrupts the silence by crackling and snapping. Seagull is dancing. She carries a gray-and-white birch-bark basket and she tilts it towards him. The basket is empty. She glides back and forth, and Many Smiles makes the fire awaken and raise its head as she moves. Seagull dances on, she circles the fire. The basket grows heavier. Seagull begins to stagger under its weight. Many Smiles begins to cry and sings a song of sadness, missing his beloved wife, and knowing that she has made her journey. She stops dancing, strokes the tear from his cheek, and smiles at him.

"Beloved, now you understand that the heaviest burden any of us ever bear is an empty basket."

"But how can I fill this emptiness?"

The fire dies down, and the wigwam grows darker and darker, until nearly all the light is gone. The drumming outside the circle stops and the wind picks up. In the wind, Many Smiles thinks he can hear the faint melody of a flute.

In the shadows, Many Smiles sees a younger version of himself. The boy takes a feather from behind his ear. "Pass it on, our teacher."

5.5 How I Got My Name:
My True Story

"Is that *really* your name? Child, I knew a man who had exactly the same name! How did you get yours?"

The young boy stands in front of the ancient Storyteller Grandfather Many Smiles.

"Would you like to hear, Storyteller? Then I will tell you how I got my whole name. Half of my name was given to me by my Grandmother Helping Hands and the other half was given to me by my Grandfather Holds Peace Strong. Their names together are a lesson and a story you know, Helping Hands Holds Peace Strong."

"I already like this story, young one. It makes me think of my own name and my wife's. I am Many Smiles, and she was Seagull. And we know that seagulls speak by laughter. So, together our names mean *We Speak Through Laughter and Many Smiles.*"

"Thank you, Grandfather. I often think of such things."

"You think like a Storyteller, little one. Continue your story."

"One day I heard a woman ask my grandmother, 'Helping Hands, who is that little boy drawing pictures on birchbark so quietly?' My grandmother answered, 'That is Still Waters Running Deep.'"

"On another day, my grandfather and I were sitting together under a tree and his men friends came by. One of them asked, 'Holds Peace Strong, who is that little boy?' And my grandfather answered, 'He is The Little Hawk That Sits By. He always sits by me and, whenever I drop something while we are walking in the tall grass, I ask him to find it for me and he goes right to it just like a hawk. So he is the Little Hawk That Sits By.'"

"When you put both names together, my whole name is The Little Hawk That Sits By Still Waters Running Deep."

"Grandson, someday, you will be a gifted Storyteller."

The young boy, Little Hawk, smiles.

5.6 *The Flight of the Turkey Vulture:*
Telling Stories that Dance in a Circle

"Grandfather, grandfather, how much farther before we reach the wigwam of Grandfather Many Smiles?"

"Grandchild, we will arrive there when our journey is over," Holds Peace Strong said, as he and his grandson, a boy named Little Hawk That Sits By Still Waters Running Deep, headed for the stream that marked the boundary between the village where Long Canoe was Chief, and the village where Two Moccasins was Chief.

Far beyond, at the Fire of the Ancestors, Grandfather Little Hawk, Grandmother Dancing Rain, and Grandmother Seagull sat together. They noticed a rare visitor: a turkey vulture, traveling on the South Wind.

Seagull spoke. "The turkey vulture travels in many worlds: the Sky World, the World of The People who Walk the Earth, and the Spirit World. But he rarely visits Our People. In my whole lifetime, I only saw him once or twice. Why do you think he never came to listen to our stories on Earth?"

Dancing Rain answered, "It is true that he travels between the worlds easily. But his head is bald and he has no hat. The place where we lived gets very cold. He prefers to stay in the South. Only sometimes, when the hot Southern Breeze reaches all the way to our shores, and the walrus swims further North, then he visits our people and listens to our stories. In fact, one night, long ago, a great Southern Storm carried him up to our island, and he perched in a fir tree. Protected from the cold rain and the winds, he listened. That night, he heard a boy calling a new name into the stormy sky."

"Shall I tell you a story?" Grandfather Little Hawk asked the turkey vulture.

The turkey vulture landed on a branch nearby.

"Here we tend the fires of the Ancestors. The hunting is good. Here we do well. Therefore, Turkey Vulture, when I have finished my story, please travel from these shores to the land of Our People, and leave your gift with them."

After the story had ended, South Wind began to blow warm breezes so that Turkey Vulture's bald head would not be cold on his journey North. Soon, soaring high in the sky, Turkey Vulture arrived in the land of Little Hawk's people.

He rested on a high branch above a wigwam, and he heard the story he'd been listening to the last time he visited these people of the North. Then he jumped into the sky. As he rose, the voices of these people rose with him. Like the vulture, the stories of The People flew in circles, rising higher, reaching generation after generation, perching, listening, then rising again.

Grandfather and grandson moved along deer trails of hot gravel. The mosquitoes danced around them. The Sun shone so brightly that the boy pulled his hair over his eyes, and imagined he was walking through a forest of thin, black vines. When the Sun was overhead, and all the animals were bedded down for a quiet time, Grandfather Holds Peace Strong led his grandson to a stream. The smooth, wet stones at the bottom of the stream bed made the boy's feet want to dance for joy and gratitude. So he danced to thank the stream and the rocks. Grandfather smiled. They drank the cold water, bathed themselves, and rested.

The day was hot for all the creatures that call our land home, but the weather was just right for the vulture.

In the Northern lands, South Wind cannot ever stay long, even to protect the bald head of the vulture. Soon, South Wind and Turkey Vulture had to return to their own places.

Turkey Vulture spread his wings as if to thank his friends for their stories. Then he left a gift that would soon fill an empty basket. Circling like a story on the warm breeze, he turned South, and flew home.

"Grandfather, Grandfather, I'd like to know if there are more cool streams further along that we can dance in, and be grateful for, and soothe our feet, and bathe in, and lie down next to."

"For now, we have this stream to be thankful for," Grandfather said.

After they rested, they walked along the stream bed, and the water was so clear that the boy could never tell if the waters ran deep or shallow. The slippery fallen logs in the stream played tricks, tripping him, and then bouncing up and down with mischievous splash-laughter. The river rocks danced under the boy's feet. In places, the current grew strong, pushing him faster.

"Grandfather, Grandfather, Grandfather..."

Grandfather lifted his finger to silence his grandson.

Between them, they didn't need words. As Holds Peace Strong watched his grandson play, a shy fox approached the stream and watched as well. The water called and the child responded to the water. He let the current lift him as he splashed and laughed, watching the ripples and waves form. As the children and the elders do so well, he told the truth about who he was. Grandfather and Grandson together filled the space around themselves with love.

Grandfather Holds Peace Strong turned back and looked along the course of the stream, where the afternoon Sun reflected in the water's movement. On the surface of the stream, was the long, dark brown, thick, perfect feather of a turkey vulture. The feather traveled quickly, skillfully maneuvering downstream around boulders and branches and heading straight for the young Storyteller named Little Hawk.

5.7 Your Story and Mine:
Letting the Story Tell YOU
and Listen to its Song

Y'Nay ha ho ne y'nay ha ho ne eey ha ho nay y'nay ha ho ne

>Then the stories age
>And they stay the same
>And they never change
>But they're not the same
>Because every day
>And from age to age
>We stay just the same
>But we're not the same
>Because stories came
>And that day we changed
>And the stories change
>us—We're not the same
>And the stories came
>From the change we made.

Y'Nay ha ho ne y'nay ha ho ne eey ha ho nay

>Then the stories age
>And they stay the same
>Generation to Generation
>By whatever name.

Six

CURRICULUM

(Frank Domenico Cipriani's words)

A word about this curriculum: When Grandmother Beverly suggested that we include this curriculum as part of our book, I questioned if this was wise. After all, the lessons in this book had already been covered in each of the stories. And now, with the proposed addition of a curriculum, I feared people would not look beyond it to find the many subtle lessons of each chapter.

Grandmother said it came down to a question of respect for different people's ways, and the fact that not everybody had the time or even the skills to search for their lessons within the stories. She suggested that I include the storytelling curriculum we had used for children in our Magic Forest program, combined with the curriculum I had developed for our upcoming course for adults, The World of the Storyteller.

Because our classes are small and custom-designed, the sequence of lessons changes, based on the needs of the students. So when I presented this curriculum chart to friends and proofreaders, everyone wanted to know what the order of the lessons was, should they follow the curriculum horizontally or vertically?

Please allow me to give you a little insight into the purpose of the curriculum. In this way, if you choose to use this section you can find find the approach that works best for you.

As you look at the chart, the first two columns deal with reading the book, first to yourself and then out loud. This is a prerequisite to our storytelling workshop. Read the book through twice, doing the exercises in vertical order on the chart, from first lesson to last lesson. If you wish, you are welcome to take the exercises and post them on our Facebook site. This way, even if you're working alone, you have an audience. Please do a search of "Learning Little Hawk's Way of Storytelling" on Facebook fan groups to find us.

Once you have completed the first two columns, the rest of the curriculum can be followed as courses: Storytelling I, Storytelling II, Storytelling III, and Storytelling IV. Now, you will need to find yourself a Caretaker, one with whom you can work throughout the learning process. Go back to the section labeled Storytelling I, and complete the next four columns working horizontally, that is, do section 2.1 completing the Outdoor Read, the sections labeled "With Caretaker", the section labeled "Larger Audience", and the section labeled "Wordless" in that order, before moving on to section 2.2. Once you complete all seven sections of Storytelling I, you will be ready to present performance pieces. Find an audience, perform these pieces, and by all means, record your best and send them to us. Repeat the course with Storytelling II, III, and IV. Once you have completed all but the last column of every section, then complete the last column from beginning to end. Teach someone else the skills of storytelling. Teaching is one of the most effective ways to learn.

The reason I designed the sections in this way, is so that student Storytellers would spend some time each day outside, some time with his/her Caretaker, and some time with a larger audience which may consist of fellow students. None of this curriculum is set in stone and, in fact, if you can come up with better lessons or helpful critique which will allow us to improve this section of the book, we welcome and encourage your comments.

However you learn these skills, we ask that you remember that the type of Storytelling we admire is not merely entertaining, but it's also uplifting.

The key to successful storytelling is sharing stories that illustrate life's magnificent empowering array of choices and enlightening ideas. It does not seek to be outrageous for the sake of entertainment or poke cruel fun and single people out for the sake of comedy. We do not lift the level of understanding when we mock groups of people. We cannot fill the room with love by using hate speech, no matter how justified we think we are.

We need to ask ourselves, not only in our stories, but in all our actions: "How will what I do today affect those who will live seven generations from now?" Tell your stories to the audience of today, but imagine how these tales will be heard far into the future.

I've had the good fortune to be born into a family that values knowledge and ability as two of the greatest treasures a human being can acquire. If you look at the cover of this book, you will see that it says *as taught to* Frank Domenico Cipriani. At the beginning of all the courses I have ever taught, I always make the same disclaimer: My triumphs belong to my teachers, my mistakes are my own. Because my parents and grandparents always taught us to search for knowledge, I have been blessed throughout my life with the most wonderful teachers imaginable. One of the main reasons why I became a writer was so that I could share the lessons that they had given me with the world.

I have written manuscripts telling the stories of lessons I've learned in many subjects. I cannot claim authorship to any of this work, except where it falls short of the level of excellence that those who originally imparted this knowledge to me were able to provide. Knowledge is one of those wonderful treasures, like kindness, that increases in quality and quantity the more often that it is shared.

That's the point of the unusual byline of this book.

If I have communicated Grandfather Little Hawk's and Grandmother Beverly's lessons successfully enough that you feel you can remove my name from the "as taught to" byline and replace it with your own, then I have succeeded as a writer.

How to use this curriculum chart

If you wish to have some structure as you learn storytelling, please feel free to use this curriculum, which we developed for our storytelling workshop. After you finish this book, if you wish to follow the curriculum, we suggest you go back and apply this while rereading the book from beginning to end. Each time you reach the end of a section, do the exercise outlined.

(continued on page 204)

Storytelling I   Play: Lessons Learned in Childhood. *Am I like a child at play?*

	First read	Read aloud	Outdoor read	With Caretaker	Larger audience	Wordless	Seventh Generation
2.1: Childhood Before Memory	Explain why you want to become a Storyteller.	Create a character who is a Storyteller. Tell someone in the character's voice why that character wants to be a Storyteller.	Find a place outdoors to play and grow as a Storyteller.	Find a Caretaker. Explain why you want to be a Storyteller. Write your impressions of your companion, and seal the impressions in an envelope.	Work on an **entrance.** Announce your intention to be a Storyteller to a group of people.	Act out your reasons for being a Storyteller using only movement and music.	Find a student who wants to become a Storyteller.
2.2: At the Village of Little Hawk and D.R.	Make a storytelling pouch and find a pebble. Play.	Play, focusing on changing voices.	Go to your outdoor place and play with the elements in nature.	Play with your Caretaker. Incorporate dialogue and humor.	Play with members of an audience or sit somewhere and observe the voice and movement of people. Practice mimicking them privately.	Play with someone using only different voices and gibberish.	Observe new Storytellers playing. Watch for self-consciousness.
2.3: My Sister the Eagle…	Think of the one moral that you would like your stories to teach.	Think about the voice with which you will deliver the moral of your story, the voice of wisdom.	Observe the stories that occur around you. What are the morals?	Discuss, with your Caretaker, an important lesson you wish to teach.	Ask a larger audience to share their wisdom and morals.	Convey a moral without using words.	Help a student discover the meaning of his/her life lessons. What do they teach *you?*

2.4: S.D. Makes A Trade…	Look up the meaning of your name. Think about the purposes of storytelling,	Say your own name or nickname in different voices. Say it with anger, love, fear etc.	Say your name or nickname to the Sky, to the Earth, does your name tell the truth about you?	Come up with an introduction and **introduce** yourself to your Caretaker.	**Introduce** your name with a song, a cadence or call and response that truly reflects who you are.	Express your name without saying it. You can use words, music, movement.	Say your student's name. Have them repeat it back to you over and over. Observe what happens.
2.5: Little Thunder's Wedding	Find a **traditional tale** of your own culture that has a moral.	Retell the **traditional tale** in your own way. Think of other traditional tales where you would change the ending.	Tell the **traditional tale** to the ants, the clouds, the trees.	Retell the **traditional tale** to your Caretaker. Ask for SNWE (South, North, West and East) critique.	Tell the **traditional tale** to a larger audience.	Tell the **traditional tale** without using understandable words.	Tell your **tale** to your student. Notice how right you want everything to be when you know you're going to be watched by your student.
2.6: Land Tells a Story	Can you remember the landmarks in the story backwards and forwards?	Use different voices for the different landmarks in the story. Imagine the story from different points of view. Does changing voices help you to remember?	**Take a walk.** Learn the landmarks. Listen to the voices of the landmarks. If they could talk how would they talk? **What is the moral of your walk?**	Describe **your walk,** backwards and forwards, to your Caretaker.	Take a group on the same **walk** you took in the other exercises in this section. Describe your interpretation of the landmarks.	Speak to a foreign group or talk gibberish and gesture to describe the landmarks you have seen on **your walk.**	Have a student lead you down a trail. Play the role of Becomes Unseen and teach the skill.
2.7: Story the Land Told M.S.	Read this story aloud.	Focus on your many voices.	"Cook up" a story from **your walk.** Make sure you include the moral of your walk.	Tell the story you cooked up from **your walk** to your Caretaker.	Tell the story of **your walk** to an audience.	Tell the story of **your walk** using only gibberish, gestures, music, and movement.	Tell the story of **your walk** to your storytelling student.

Performance pieces: Your Entrance, the Introduction of Your Name, One Traditional Tale, the Story the Land Told You (the story of your walk). Arrange a performance which includes these pieces.

Storytelling II

Lifting the Understanding: Lessons of Coming of Age. Does my understanding of the people improve during the storytelling? Does theirs improve as they spend time with me?

	First read	Read aloud	Outdoor read	With Caretaker	Larger audience	Wordless	Seventh Generation
3.1: We Have Many Faces	Picture Little Hawk, Dancing Rain, and Seagull's reaction in the story.	Read aloud. Focus on how Many Smiles' feelings would change his voice.	Vary your awareness. Tell a story to the trees, the ants, and especially to the clouds, and especially to the birds.	Do your introduction or read this story of Many Smiles to your Caretaker. Keep him/her engaged.	Imagine that your audience consists of three-year-olds. Focus on each person and keep him/her engaged.	Tell a story using gibberish. Make your audience feel sad, laugh, jump, and learn a moral.	Observe and teach a student to react with the "correct" energy.
3.2: The Best Fish	Observe how not revealing things builds anticipation.	Read this story aloud, using different narrator voices.	Notice how ground, sky, and your thoughts interact. Develop a braided story with a moral that expresses what you observe on the ground, in the sky, and inside you.	Tell your braided story to your Caretaker. Take a moral related to your life, and find three tales. Rework them so they have the same moral. Parade them together.	Tell your braided story to a larger audience.	Use words for only one of the plot lines, as you tell your braided story. Use gesture, music, and movement for the other two plot lines.	Explain braided stories to a student.
3.3: Three Stories	Go through some of your older possessions. Think of the stories each one tells.	Gather items and let them speak. Do they develop a story?	Find elements on the landscape and wait for them to tell you stories. Practice these item stories (at least three).	Focus on audience reactions: restless, bored, engaged. Critique storytelling.	As Caretaker, "read" the audience and hand the Storyteller the item to cue the story that best suits the audience.	Can each item story be danced? Can it be told in music? How does tempo affect the audience?	Observe a student's interaction with his/her Caretaker. Critique South, North, West, East (SNWE).

3.4: The Feeling Lesson	Be aware of what you are feeling as you read this story.	Read aloud with a drumbeat. Be aware of how your voice changes with the drumbeat. Be aware of your feelings.	Reflect what the land is feeling. With your Caretaker, express this feeling in movement and song.	Be the drummer or Storyteller. Without consciously changing the drumbeat, just share feelings with your Storyteller/Caretaker.	Reflect the emotional energy of a group of people. Use body, voice, hand, movement and eyes. Can you influence it by reflecting it?	Be aware how your energy affects a crowd. Try this at a sporting event. Does knowledge of a sport effect ability to influence energy?
3.5: Eastern-Facing Story	As you read, think about how anticipation increases awareness.	Try and imitate sounds that surround you as they occur.	Call the sunrise to you. Anticipate it with every cell of your being. "Pull the dawn" into the sky.	Caretake someone's fire, as they tell an Eastern-Facing Story.	Make the audience notice its surroundings. Use anticipation, silence, and movement.	**Improve your entrance.** Use fire, music, and movement to build anticipation.
3.6: Our Many Children	Imagine the voices in the story. Close your eyes and really picture them with all your senses.	Say the story aloud. Imagine other characters. Play the story with your stone and pouch.	Using items found outdoors, create a tiny "menagerie" and create voices for the menagerie.	Take turns singing a call and responding. Pick creatures from your menagerie and call and respond in their voices.	Tell one of your stories using puppets or toys.	Speak in gibberish, and have audiences guess which creature belongs to which voice. Don't use "realistic" animal noises.
3.7: What Fire Taught Us	Picture how you might create the elements described in the story.	Experiment with light and positioning in a storytelling area. How does it affect mood?	Practice with fire. How big a fire is necessary for your story?	Caretake someone else's fire. Become familiar enough with the other person's stories so that your fire responds to the story.	With your Caretaker, tell an evening of stories around a fire. Take turns focusing on the caretaking of the fire.	Do a night of fire and storytelling using only music, movement and voice to tell your stories.

3.4: The Feeling Lesson	Attend a game or crowded venue with a student. Feel the energy of the crowd and reflect that energy.
3.5: Eastern-Facing Story	Be the Sun in the Eastern-Facing Story for your student.
3.6: Our Many Children	Play the animal call and response character game with your student.
3.7: What Fire Taught Us	With your Caretaker, create an exemplary storytelling for students.

Performance pieces: Braided Story, three "item" stories, Improved Entrance.

Storytelling III   **Telling the Truth: Lessons from Adulthood.** *Do my stories reflect my authentic self?*

	First read	Read aloud	Outdoor read	With Caretaker	Larger audience	Wordless	Seventh Generation
4.1: The Shortest Story	Tell your **shortest life story**. Include your name and no more than five other words.	Notice the different points of view and the many voices of the shortest story.	Close your eyes. Open them for 3 seconds What's happening? Create a story with a moral out of what you see.	Tell the same **shortest story** as another Storyteller/Caretaker. Note similarities and differences in style.	Tell your **shortest story** to an audience.	Can you tell the **shortest story** with no words at all? Can you tell it in another language?	Ask a student to come up with a five-word story. Can you braid your story with your student's?
4.2: The Great Preparation	Read the story. How would you fill the space? What props would you make for your own story?	Fill a big space and a little space with your voice.	How does nature fill space? How big a "shadow" does a bird or an insect control? How does a mosquito or a cricket or a tree capture your attention?	Caretake another person's storytelling. Be aware of the audience and direct your storytelling to fill the space.	In front of a big audience, fill the space with the help of your Caretaker.	In front of an audience, fill a space wordlessly using only movement, music and sound.	Observe another Storyteller or if available, a two-year-old in a family setting. Learn how the child or the other Storyteller fills his/her space.
4.3: Seagull Breaks Her Leg	How did Seagull fill the space? How would you fill it?	Roll three dice and multiply the results. With each paragraph, speak the story as if you were talking to people that are the same age as your results.	Without moving from where you're sitting, What is the most distant element in nature that affects you? What is the most distant one that you affect?	Together with your Caretaker, act as if you have broken your leg and have to fill a room. Tell one of your stories.	Develop "props" to hand out to your audience. The props should be numerous.	How would you, as a Caretaker, wordlessly direct the audience to use the props?	Show a student how to fill space. For purposes of teaching, create obstacles for yourself

4.4: 'The Turkey Vulture Feather'	Think about the feather exercise. Would you be able to tell the truth?	Tell the truth about yourself using the voices of your menagerie. Does this create a comic effect?	Tell your most difficult truths to nature. First to nature around you, and then if you dare, to the stars and moon.	Pass the feather and tell the truth to your Caretaker.	Use a hard **truth** in your **story**, in the third person. Create a moral to the story. Critique with SNWE method.	Tell your **truth story** using music, voice, and call and respond it with your Caretaker	Exchange the truth with a student in an appropriate way. Critique SNWE.
4.5: A Story of Understanding	How could you apply the principles in the story to understand physical or emotional pain?	How many points of view are there in this story?	Pretend you're injured. Practice a Story of Understanding. How does understanding relate to telling the truth?	Tell the truth about a place where you're hurting. Practice the Story of Understanding.	How would you tell a Story of Understanding in a hospital ward? Nursing home?	How would you tell a Story of Understanding to someone who doesn't understand your language?	Tell a Story of Understanding to a student.
4.6: Helping Hands	Could you find stories in tracks? What truths do your surroundings tell about you?	Picture the tracks that Helping Hands would leave before and after his change of heart.	Create the tracks of fanciful creatures, animals, and people of different ages, then study the tracks.	Go tracking with your Caretaker. Ask, "What creatures live here? How do they move? What happens on this landscape?"	Take one of your stories and practice making the tracks the characters would make. Observe how this affects your movement.	Using paper cutouts if you're indoors, create a **story that's all track**, ie., Footprint, footprint, dropped feather, footprint on the ceiling.	Have a student look at his/her own tracks, and explain what they illustrate about him/her.
4.7: Always the Same, Always	Think about the story and where personality comes through in the dialogue.	How would you precisely imitate a comedian or Storyteller you know?	Don't go to your usual place to read this story. Find a different natural environment. How does that affect you?	**Borrow a story**, getting the appropriate permission. Adapt it to your own truth.	Create a ten-word story to honor the person you **borrowed** the **story** from.	Make your **borrowed story** work through tracks, through effects, through music and movement, without words.	Create a story as a gift to a student. You need to know the student well enough to give him/her an appropriate story.

Performance pieces: The Shortest Story, A Truth Story, A Story That's All Track, A Borrowed Story.

Storytelling IV   Filling the Space with Love: The Wisdom of the Ancestors.

Do I treat the people in my audience like beloved relatives? Do they feel my love?

	First read	Read aloud	Outdoor read	With Caretaker	Larger audience	Wordless	Seventh Generation
5.1: The Oldest Storyteller	Read and reflect how the way you dress speaks about you.	Look at your own wardrobe. Who lives in these clothes? What stories do these clothes tell? How many of these clothes are chosen with love?	What elements from your special outdoor place can you incorporate into your storytelling garments?	Prepare storytelling clothing. Have your Caretaker guess the story of your outfit.	Create one outfit that tells a story, your introduction or five-word story. Have someone look at the outfit and tell you the story they think it tells.	Look at your outfit with a critical eye. How well does it transcend literal meaning? How universal is it?	Critique your student's wardrobe using SNWE.
5.2: Carry a Lighter Burden	What are the many layers of lesson in this story?	What are the lessons that the different points of view teach in this story?	Quiet your thoughts and become aware. Listen.	Sit in silence with your Caretaker. Just be aware.	Observe the power of darkness and silence in a performance.	In darkness and silence, reach out for the "feeling" in a room of people.	Share a time of silence with a student. Critique that silence SNWE.
5.3: Words Don't Need to be Understood	How would you prepare a story for a dog? A bird?	Read this story critically. What could you cut from this story to make it better?	Look for an insect, a bird or some other animal. Tell your story responding to their reactions and movement.	Can you make your story understood to your Caretaker although it was designed to communicate with an animal or plant?	Tell your story to creation itself. All the plants and animals are your audience. React to your audience and respond.	Create a **story based on silence.**	Using a drum, tell a student you love them without words, movement or facial expression.

5.4: The Vulture Feather	How would you assess your editing ability in a story? Do you go on too long?	Imagine how your great-grandchild would tell the story of who you are.	Tell a story to an insect or quickly passing bird. Tell it before it flies away.	Tell your Caretaker a story. Time it. Tell it in half the time. Repeat until story is too short to have meaning.	Tell a story in as little time as possible. Spend most of the time responding to your audience.	Use one minute to relay the moral of your story. Use only props, music or movement.	Pare down a familiar fairytale. Keep subtracting one minute from the story.
5.5: How I Got My Name	Whom do you honor by being a Storyteller? What are your own roots?	Think about a great-grandchild of yours telling the story of whom you were.	Look at the land. What has your presence contributed to *its* next Generation?	Come up with a team name for you and your Caretaker. Tell the **story of the team name** with fire, dance, music, and both your voices.	Do the same character types keep showing up in your audience? Invent names for these character types.	Use a sound or movement to express the essence of one of your audience members.	Nickname your student using a SNWE critique.
5.6: Flight of the Turkey Vulture	Explain to someone why you want to be a Storyteller.	Create a deeper level to the character you are as a Storyteller. Tell someone in that character's voice why you became a Storyteller.	Go outside and play with your stone and pouch.	Allow your student to become a second Caretaker to you. Explain why the other wanted to become a Storyteller.	Work on an entrance. Tell the story of your **storytelling journey** as a story with a moral.	Act out your **storytelling journey** without using words.	Help your student find a student.
5.7: Your Story and Mine	This book is in your hands. Where are you? Where has this book brought you? Let us know, please.	Speak for this book. What would it tell you if it could come to life for one minute?	The landscape is the same landscape but it changes and you change. How have you and your special place remained the same since you first saw it?	You were asked to write the impressions of your Caretaker and seal those impressions in an envelope. Read those impressions now.	In your performance, be aware of your first impression of the audience and the impression by the end of the performance. Has this stayed the same?	Note how your own body and breathing communicates with you. In a mirror, act out your **storytelling journey.**	You are my teacher. Please critique our lessons, SNWE

Performance pieces: Story Based on Silence, Story of your team name, Your Storytelling Journey.

In our workshops, we would follow the curriculum differently: we'd have the students read all the stories twice through and do the first two columns of all the exercises before coming to the workshop. Then, for Storytelling I, for instance, we focused on chapters 2.1–2.7, following each exercise in the section vertically through the chart.

As you do each exercise, ask yourself the key question of the section, which is in the heading of each section. For instance, the central question for Storytelling I is, *Am I like a child at play?* At the end of each section, the Storyteller should be able to present the stories labeled *Performance Pieces*.

Consider these exercises mere suggestions. See how many more exercises you can glean from the stories themselves. The items in bold lettering indicate individual stories you will be developing into performance pieces. So, for instance, when we mention a **traditional tale**, we invite you to use the same **traditional tale** for all exercises, in order to polish your telling of this single tale into a fine performance. Each time you choose a new **traditional tale** to tell, follow each of the exercises again.

If you want to learn more about the storytelling workshops offered, please visit: www.kennethlittlehawk.com

Seven

The Relatedness of the Characters
And Acknowledgements

Startle Drumming a.k.a. Many Smiles' Childhood Village:

Great-Great-Grandparents:
* Red Branch (F): Aunt of Two Heartbeat
  Thanks for your support, Pam.

Great-Grandparents:
* Two Heartbeat (F): Clan Mother, Mother of Deer Cloud
  Special thanks to author Nan Marino for helping in the early days of this book.

* Two Wolves (M): Chief of Startle Drumming's village
  Special thanks for your support, Kfir.

Grandparents:
* Deer Cloud (M): Grandfather of Startle Drumming
* Painted Sky (F): Village Puoin
  Thanks to Frank's Mom for reading the stories.

Parents and Uncles:
* Becomes Unseen (M): Uncle of Many Smiles

Children and Grandchildren:
* Startle Drumming a.k.a. Many Smiles (M): Husband of Seagull
* Circling Eagle (M): Cousin of Many Smile's
  A tribute to our friend of the same name.

Dancing Rain/Little Hawk's Village:

Great-Great Grandparents:
• Keeps Watch (M): Paternal Grandfather of Little Hawk and Dancing Rain (in Braided Story)
• Snow Moved by Wind (F): Grandmother of Little Hawk and Dancing Rain (in Braided Story)
   Thanks to Ramya Sarma for looking over the manuscript.

• Singing Whale (M): Maternal Grandfather of Little Hawk (in What Fire Taught Us)
   Thanks to Jean for helping us with HM's work.

Grandparents (Siblings):
• Little Hawk (M): Great-Uncle of Seagull
• Dancing Rain(F): Grandmother of Seagull

Other Grandparents:
• Talking Leaves (M): Keeper of the Flame
   Tribute to our friend, who was Firekeeper and former Chief for his Lenape band, and a fine craftsman of regalia.

• Silver Eagle (M): Chief of Little Hawk's clan, Father of One Moccasin
• Little Dove (F): Wife of Silver Eagle and Clan Mother
   Tribute to our friend Silver Eagle, the Grand Chief of the Métis of Maine, and Grand Council Member, Little Dove.

Parents and Parents' Generation:
• Gray Dog (F): Mother of Seagull and Puoin
   Thanks to Julie of Practical Primitive for the photo sessions and support, and to dear Hugo.

• Howling Wolf (M): Father of Seagull and Puoin
• One Moccasin (M): Chief candidate to the new village
• Little Bow (M): Father of Sea Mink
• Playful Otter a.k.a. Seagull (F): Storyteller and wife of Many Smiles
   Thanks for listening in the early going, Emma, and adding your suggestions.

Great-Grandchildren:
• Two Moccasins (M): Grandson of One Moccasin, successor to the Chief
   Thanks to our cover designer Richard Crookes.

New Village

Grandparents:
• Becomes Unseen (M): Chief

Parents:
• Seagull (F), Many Smiles (M)

Children:
• Long Canoe (M): Son of Many Smiles and Seagull. Second Chief of village
Thanks to Eddie and Practical Primitive for all the technical and moral support.

• Quiet Claw (F): Daughter of Many Smiles and Seagull and Puoin of the village
Thanks to Mária for making this book conform to the style sheet.

Acknowledgements through character names:

Thanks to our wonderful agent Ann G. Devlin (Mountain Flower), Frank's son, Domenico (Yellow Wing), John Pritchard's School of Digital Arts (Thunder Bear), Sabine Weeke (Spotted Shorttail), Gail Torr (Wind Storm), and Louise (Wind Walks Woman) Barton for the epic rescue of our words. And we would also like to thank Shari Mueller (Healing Water), for the catches she made. We dedicate this book to all our relatives, all of you who have shared our stories.

We thank some of those who have helped us by dedicating characters to them. However, any connection between the fictitious characters in this book and any actual person, living or deceased, is entirely coincidental.

FINDHORN PRESS

Life-Changing Books

For a complete catalogue,
please contact:

Findhorn Press Ltd
117–121 High Street
Forres IV36 1AB
Scotland, UK

t +44(0)1309 690582
f +44(0)131 777 2711
e info@findhornpress.com

or consult our catalogue online
(with secure order facility) on
www.findhornpress.com

For information on the Findhorn Foundation:
www.findhorn.org